Literacy by Design

Assessment Guide
Theme Progress Tests and Test Practice

Rigby®

A Harcourt Achieve Imprint

www.Rigby.com
1-800-531-5015

Contents

Using This Book

Ongoing Test Practice

Ongoing Test Practice provides students with new reading passages and questions on which to practice the current theme's skills.

- Give the Ongoing Test Practice as homework after Lesson 7 of each theme.
- Make a transparency of the passage and questions to do more in-depth standardized test practice.
- Home letters in English and Spanish explain how to help children complete the test.
- Use the Answer Key on page 178 of this book to score the Ongoing Test Practice.

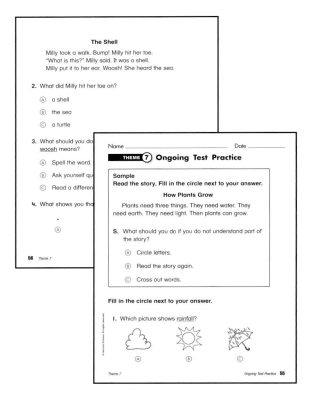

Theme Progress Tests

Theme Progress Tests cover skills and content from the student materials for each theme: comprehension, target skills, vocabulary, phonics, writing, and grammar.

- Administer the Theme Progress Test on the last day of each theme.
- For themes 1–4, read aloud all direction lines, passages, questions, and answer choices. Students should fill in the answer choice bubbles.
- For themes 5–8, read aloud all direction lines, passages, and questions. Students should read the answer choices and fill in the bubbles.
- For themes 9–16, read aloud all direction lines. Students should read the passages, questions, and answer choices and fill in the bubbles.
- Use the Student Test Record to determine students' scores using the answer key provided. Use reteaching suggestions provided at the end of each test if students score below the Criterion Score.

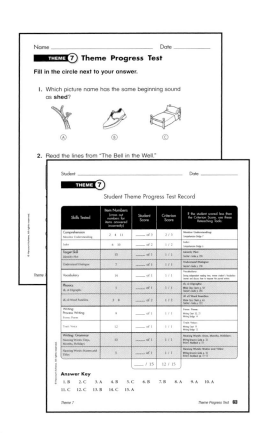

Mid-Year and End-of-Year Reviews

The Mid-Year and End-of-Year Reviews provide cumulative assessments. Students practice taking tests using new reading passages.

- The Student Test Record at the end of each test allows for easy scoring and provides reteaching suggestions.

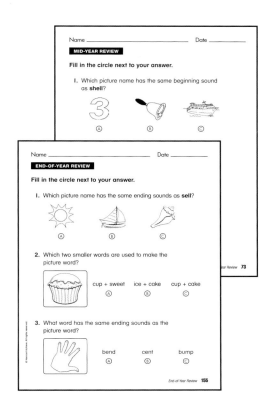

High-Frequency Word Assessments

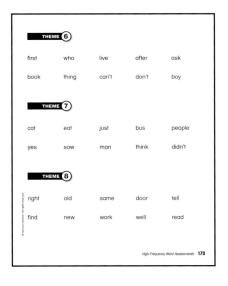

High-Frequency Word Assessments test the child's recognition of the current theme's high-frequency words (10 words per theme).

- Administer the High-Frequency Word Assessment at the end of each theme.
- Use the High-Frequency Word Assessment Tracking Form on page 177 to record the words students did not recognize and make notes about student responses.

Using Rigby READS for Reading Level Placement

Ease of Student Placement

The Rigby READS (Reading Evaluation and Diagnostic System) is a valid and reliable assessment that can be administered to the whole class in a single day. On the basis of this quick and easy assessment, teachers receive the following information.

- **Placement** Each student's individual reading level for initial instruction

- **Diagnostic** A five-pillar diagnostic that pinpoints strengths and development areas in comprehension, phonics, phonemic awareness, fluency, and vocabulary

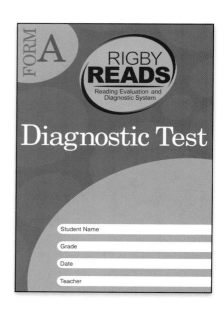

This invaluable resource is built right into the *Literacy by Design* program. Forms A and B allow you to determine end-of-year progress. The chart below shows how the Rigby READS reading levels correlate to the *Literacy by Design* reading levels.

Rigby READS Reading Level Correlation

Rigby READS Reading Level	Literacy by Design Reading Level	Rigby READS Reading Level	Literacy by Design Reading Level
Early Readiness	A	2.4	M
Kindergarten	B	3.1	N
1.1	C	3.2	O
1.2	D	3.3	P
1.3	E	4.1	Q
1.4	F	4.2	R
1.5	G	4.3	S
1.6	H	5.1	T
1.7	I	5.2	U
2.1	J	5.2	V
2.2	K	6.1	W
2.3	L		

Dear Family,

Your child will be bringing home two pages of reading test practice for each theme. These activities are designed to provide practice in applying the skills learned in class in a standardized test format. We have completed the Sample passage and question together in class, so your child should be familiar with how to complete the questions on the test.

At the beginning of the year, you will need to read most of the test aloud to your child. As the year progresses, your child will read more of the test on his or her own.

Themes 1-4 (Beginning): Read aloud all direction lines, passages, questions, and answer choices. Your child should fill in the bubble for his or her answer choice.

Themes 5-8 (Mid-year): Read aloud all direction lines, passages, and questions. Your child should read the answer choices himself or herself and fill in the bubble for his or her answer choice.

Themes 9-16 (End-of-year): Read aloud all direction lines. Your child should read passages, questions, and answer choices himself or herself and fill in the bubble for his or her answer choice.

Teacher: _____

Estimada familia,

Su hijo/a llevará a casa dos páginas de práctica para la prueba de lectura de cada tema. El objectivo de estas actividades es proporcionar práctica en la aplicación de las habilidades que aprendió en clase en un formato de prueba estándar. Hemos terminado el ejemplo de pasaje y la pregunta juntos en clase, por lo que su hijo/a deberá conocer bien en contestar las preguntas en la prueba.

Al comenzar del año, necesitará leerle la mayoría de la prueba en voz alta a su hijo/a. Al avanzar el año, su hijo/a podrá leer más de la prueba por sí solo/a.

Temas 1-4 (Al principio): Lee en voz alta todas las instrucciones, los pasajes, las preguntas y las opciones de la respuesta. Su hijo/a deberá llenar el círculo con su opción de la respuesta.

Temas 5-8 (Medio año): Lee en voz alta todas las instrucciones, los pasajes y las preguntas. Su hijo/a deberá leer las opciones de la respuesta sin ayuda y llenar el círculo con su opción de la respuesta.

Temas 9-16 (Fin del año): Lee en voz alta todas las instrucciones. Su hijo/a deberá leer los pasajes, las preguntas y las opciones de la respuesta sin ayuda y llenar el círculo con su opción de la respuesta.

Maestro/a: _____

Filling in a Circle

On a test, you may need to fill in a circle. This is how you show your answer. Fill in the circle next to the best answer. Fill in the circle completely.

Look at the circles on this page. Only the first one shows the right way to fill in an answer circle.

This is the way to fill in the circle. Fill it in completely.

This is not the way. Do not use a check mark. Fill in the circle completely.

This is not the way. Do not write an "X" in the circle. Fill in the circle completely.

This is not the way. Do not fill in part of the circle. Fill in the circle completely.

Let's Practice!

Fill in each circle completely.

    1. ◯

    2. ◯

    3. ◯

Fill in the circle next to the letter A.

    Ⓐ   A

    Ⓑ   B

    Ⓒ   C

Fill in the circle next to the letter B.

    Ⓐ   A

    Ⓑ   B

    Ⓒ   C

Fill in the circle below the letter C.

A	B	C
Ⓐ	Ⓑ	Ⓒ

I. Fill in the circle next to the **dog**.

Ⓐ

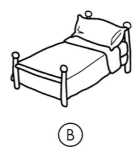
Ⓑ

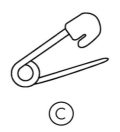
Ⓒ

2. Fill in the circle next to the **clock**.

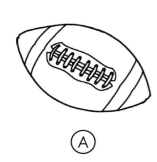
Ⓐ

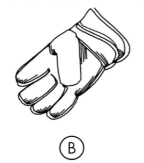
Ⓑ

Ⓒ

3. Fill in the circle next to the **five**.

Ⓐ

Ⓑ

Ⓒ

4. Fill in the circle next to the **car**.

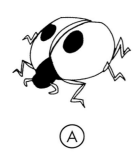
Ⓐ

Ⓑ

Ⓒ

X *Bubbling Practice*

Name _____ Date _____

Sample
Read the story. Fill in the circle next to your answer.

A Letter to Jada

Dear Jada,

　　Please come to my house. We can play in the
backyard. Mom will make ham. Yum! We will have fun!

Your friend,
Chad

S. What else will Chad and Jada do besides play?

work	eat	sleep
Ⓐ	Ⓑ	Ⓒ

Fill in the circle next to your answer.

I. What word has the same middle sound as the picture word?

had	cut	hen
Ⓐ	Ⓑ	Ⓒ

2. Choose the word that belongs on the line.

Ann let Van use her crayons. Ann likes to _____.

pen   share   blue

Ⓐ   Ⓑ   Ⓒ

Make a Snack

Get butter and jam. Get bread.
Put butter on bread. Put jam on bread. Put the parts together. Cut in two. Eat!

---

3. What do you need to cut the sandwich?

      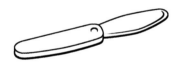

Ⓐ   Ⓑ   Ⓒ

4. What goes well with this snack?

Ⓐ   Ⓑ   Ⓒ

Name _____   Date _____

Fill in the circle next to your answer.

1. What word has the same ending sounds as the picture word?

hot	fig	tan
Ⓐ	Ⓑ	Ⓒ

2. Read the lines from "The Bear Who Wouldn't Share."

> I know! I'll only ask those friends who won't fit through my door!

What kind of friends will Bear invite?

big	brown	little
Ⓐ	Ⓑ	Ⓒ

3. Which picture name has the same middle sound as the first picture name?

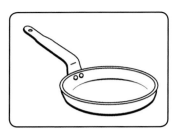

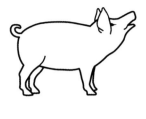
Ⓐ

Ⓑ

Ⓒ

4. Which is a sentence?

Ⓐ   runs fast

Ⓑ   happy

Ⓒ   I eat apples.

5. Which two words rhyme?

ran, man

man, mat

rug, ran

Ⓐ

Ⓑ

Ⓒ

6. Which sentence has good word order?

Ⓐ   Ate bear cake.

Ⓑ   Cake bear ate.

Ⓒ   Bear ate cake.

7. What does the word <u>cooperate</u> mean?

Tad will <u>cooperate</u> with Ali on the painting.

Ⓐ work together

Ⓑ clean

Ⓒ hold the paintbrush

8. What should you do **first** when you write?

Ⓐ Share.

Ⓑ Think of ideas.

Ⓒ Fix your writing.

9. Which picture name has the same middle sound as **nap**?

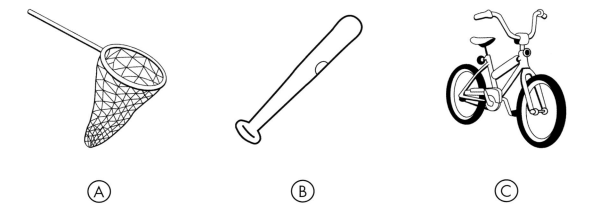

Ⓐ   Ⓑ   Ⓒ

10. Read the lines from "The Bear Who Wouldn't Share."

> Push! Shove!
> Push some more!
> Oh dear, I can't fit through my door!
> Bear suddenly felt very left out.

How did Bear feel when this happened?

Ⓐ happy

Ⓑ excited

Ⓒ sad

11. What word shows when something happens in a story?

Ⓐ over

Ⓑ and

Ⓒ first

12. Read the lines from "The Bear Who Wouldn't Share."

> Bear suddenly felt very left out.
> Oh, no! I've made a big mistake.
> My friends mean more than birthday cake!

What makes "The Bear Who Wouldn't Share" make-believe?

Ⓐ   A bear is talking.

Ⓑ   A bear is eating.

Ⓒ   A bear is walking.

13. Read the lines from "The Secret."

> I have lots of friends,
> But I'm happy to share.
> I'll tell you my secret. I really don't mind.
> It's easy, said Dottie,
> Just smile and be kind!

How does Dottie look when she meets someone new?

Ⓐ

Ⓑ

Ⓒ

14. Read the lines from "The Bear Who Wouldn't Share."

> Invite your friends to tea, young Bear. I made this cake for you to share.
> It was Moose and Hippo at the door.
> Push! Shove!
> Push some more!

Why did Moose and Hippo push the door?

Ⓐ The door was broken.

Ⓑ They wanted to come in and have cake.

Ⓒ Bear was pushing them.

15. Which two words rhyme?

    sat, sob   pat, sat   pat, pit

       Ⓐ   Ⓑ   Ⓒ

Student _____ Date _____

Student Theme Progress Test Record

Skills Tested	Item Numbers (cross out numbers for items answered incorrectly)	Student Score	Criterion Score	If the student scored less than the Criterion Score, use these Reteaching Tools:
Comprehension Make Connections	2 10 13 14	_____ of 4	3 / 4	**Make Connections:** Comprehension Bridge 1
Target Skill Distinguish Fantasy from Reality	12	_____ of 1	1 / 1	**Distinguish Fantasy from Reality:** Teacher's Guide p. 16
Vocabulary	7	_____ of 1	1 / 1	**Vocabulary:** During independent reading time, review student's Vocabulary Journal and discuss how to improve the journal entries
Phonics Words with Short *a*	3 9	_____ of 2	1 / 2	**Words with Short *a*:** Whole Class Charts p. 4 Teacher's Guide p. 8
at, *an* Word Families	1 5 15	_____ of 3	2 / 3	***at*, *an* Word Families:** Whole Class Charts p. 9 Teacher's Guide p. 24
Writing: Process Writing Organizational Pattern: Sequence	11	_____ of 1	1 / 1	**Organizational Pattern: Sequence:** Writing Chart 2, 3 Writing Bridge 2
Writing Process: Introduction	8	_____ of 1	1 / 1	**Writing Process: Introduction:** Writing Chart 1 Writing Bridge 1
Writing: Grammar Words Make Sentences; Word Spacing	4	_____ of 1	1 / 1	**Words Make Sentences; Word Spacing:** Writing Resource Guide p. 1 Writer's Handbook p. 4
Word Order (Subject, Verb, Object)	6	_____ of 1	1 / 1	**Word Order (Subject, Verb, Object):** Writing Resource Guide p. 2 Writer's Handbook p. 5
		_____ / 15	12 / 15	

Answer Key

1. C   2. A   3. B   4. C   5. A   6. C   7. A   8. B   9. B   10. C

11. C   12. A   13. A   14. B   15. B

Name _____ Date _____

Sample
Read the story. Fill in the circle next to your answer.

A Good Pet

A cat is a good pet. A cat plays. A cat sleeps. A cat is loving. A cat is clean.

S. What can you ask to learn more about cats?

Ⓐ   Is a dog a good pet?

Ⓑ   What does a cat eat?

Ⓒ   What do fish eat?

Fill in the circle next to your answer.

1. What word has the same middle sound as the picture word?

nod   sit   cap

Ⓐ   Ⓑ   Ⓒ

2. Which of the following is a <u>schedule</u>?

 A

 B

Ⓒ

In the Car

Tom yells, "I want my hat!"

Pam says, "No!"

Dad stops the car. He is mad. "What is the rule?" Dad asks.

"Be nice," says Tom.

"Be nice," says Pam.

---

3. What can you ask as you read about Tom and Pam?

Ⓐ   How should they act in the car?

Ⓑ   What color is the hat?

Ⓒ   What school does Tom go to?

4. What can you ask as you read about Dad?

Ⓐ   What kind of car does Dad drive?

Ⓑ   Does Dad wear a hat?

Ⓒ   What rule does Dad have?

Name _____   Date _____

Fill in the circle next to your answer.

1. Which picture name has the same ending sounds as the first picture?

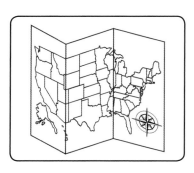 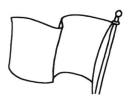 

                                       Ⓐ   Ⓑ   Ⓒ

2. Read the lines from "Play Long Ago."

> Long ago, some children played with marbles.
> Some children played with dolls.

What can you ask to learn more about what children played with?

Ⓐ   What other games did children play?

Ⓑ   What clothes did children wear?

Ⓒ   Where did children buy marbles?

3. Which two words rhyme?

tap, lap   top, tap   lap, lot

Ⓐ   Ⓑ   Ⓒ

4. Which sentence has a complete thought?

Ⓐ   Todd sat on a rock.

Ⓑ   A big rock.

Ⓒ   Todd and Tim.

5. Which picture name has the same middle sound as **job**?

Ⓐ   Ⓑ   Ⓒ

6. Which sentence is correct?

Ⓐ   the pan is hot.

Ⓑ   The pan is hot.

Ⓒ   the pan is Hot.

7. What does the word <u>yesterday</u> mean?

Today it is cold. <u>Yesterday</u> it was hot.

Ⓐ right now

Ⓑ outside

Ⓒ in the past

8. What is important when you are writing?

Ⓐ neat and clear writing

Ⓑ big pictures

Ⓒ ideas that are not in good order

9. Read the lines from "Schools Then and Now."

> Long ago, schools had very few supplies. The whole school had only one map and one blackboard.

Which picture shows something used in schools long ago and now?

  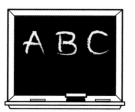

10. Which picture name has the same ending sounds as **tag**?

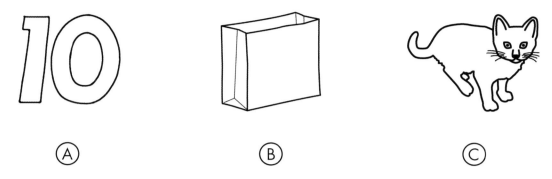

Ⓐ   Ⓑ   Ⓒ

11. Read the lines from "Schools Then and Now."

> Today towns have more people, which means more students. They have bigger schools and lots of classrooms.

What can you ask to learn more about schools today?

Ⓐ   How many classrooms do schools have today?

Ⓑ   Where is the school on a map?

Ⓒ   Do you walk home from school?

12. Choose the words that go on the line.

A report has _____.

(A) talking animals

(B) make-believe characters

(C) facts about people and things

13. Read the lines from "Schools Then and Now."

> Long ago, some children traveled many miles to get an education. They walked or rode in wagons.

What can you ask to learn more about how children travel to school?

(A) What do children learn at school?

(B) How do children get to school today?

(C) What color is a wagon?

14. Read the line from "Play Long Ago." Look at the picture.

Some children enjoyed playing stickball.

What game played today is like the game stickball?

basketball   baseball   swimming

Ⓐ   Ⓑ   Ⓒ

15. What word has the same middle sound as the picture word?

hit   hat   hot

Ⓐ   Ⓑ   Ⓒ

THEME ②

Student Theme Progress Test Record

Skills Tested	Item Numbers (cross out numbers for items answered incorrectly)	Student Score	Criterion Score	If the student scored less than the Criterion Score, use these Reteaching Tools:
Comprehension Ask Questions	2 11 13	_____ of 3	2 / 3	**Ask Questions:** Comprehension Bridge 2
Make Connections	9 14	_____ of 2	1 / 2	**Make Connections:** Comprehension Bridge 1
Vocabulary	7	_____ of 1	1 / 1	**Vocabulary:** During independent reading time, review student's Vocabulary Journal and discuss how to improve the journal entries
Phonics *ag, ap* Word Families	1 3 10	_____ of 3	2 / 3	***ag, ap* Word Families:** Whole Class Charts p. 13 Teacher's Guide p. 40
Words with Short *o*	5 15	_____ of 2	1 / 2	**Words with Short *o*:** Whole Class Charts p. 18 Teacher's Guide p. 56
Writing: Process Writing Form: Report	12	_____ of 1	1 / 1	**Form: Report:** Writing Chart 5, 6 Writing Bridge 4
Writing Traits: Introduction	8	_____ of 1	1 / 1	**Writing Traits: Introduction:** Writing Chart 4 Writing Bridge 3
Writing: Grammar Complete Sentence: Has a Complete Thought	4	_____ of 1	1 / 1	**Complete Sentence: Has a Complete Thought:** Writing Resource Guide p. 3 Writer's Handbook p. 4
Complete Sentence: Begins with a Capital Letter	6	_____ of 1	1 / 1	**Complete Sentence: Begins with a Capital Letter:** Writing Resource Guide p. 4 Writer's Handbook p. 4
		_____ / 15	11 / 15	

Answer Key

1. C   2. A   3. A   4. A   5. B   6. B   7. C   8. A   9. C   10. B

11. A   12. C   13. B   14. B   15. C

Name _____ Date _____

THEME ③ Ongoing Test Practice

Sample
Read the story. Fill in the circle next to your answer.

On the Bus

Pat gets on the bus. She sits with Tom. The bus takes them to school.

S. Which picture tells you about the story?

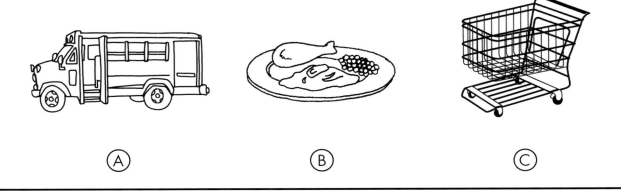

Ⓐ   Ⓑ   Ⓒ

Fill in the circle next to your answer.

1. Which picture name has the same ending sounds as the word in the box?

          Ⓐ   Ⓑ   Ⓒ

Theme 3   *Ongoing Test Practice* **19**

Ruff's New Hat

Pop the dog had a box.
"What is in the box, Pop?" asked Ruff the dog.
"Yap!" said Pop. "Open it."
"It is a new hat!" said Ruff. "Thanks, Pop! Yap! Yap!"

2. How do you know this story could not really happen?

    (A)   Ruff has a dad.

    (B)   Dogs can't talk like people.

    (C)   The dog's name is Ruff.

3. How did Ruff feel when he opened the box?

    (A)   (B)   (C)

4. Which picture tells you about the story?

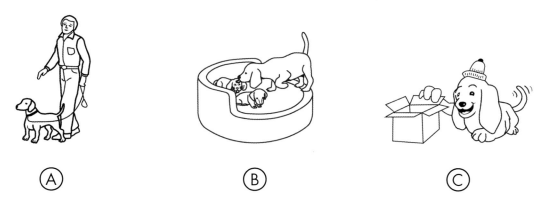

    (A)   (B)   (C)

THEME ③ Theme Progress Test

Fill in the circle next to your answer.

1. What can help you see a story in your mind?

Ⓐ   reading fast

Ⓑ   making an imaginary picture

Ⓒ   looking at the page numbers

2. Choose the word that belongs on the line.

I know the _____ to the question.

answer   motion   investigate

Ⓐ   Ⓑ   Ⓒ

3. Which picture name has the same middle sound as **zip**?

Ⓐ   Ⓑ   Ⓒ

4. Read the lines from the song "Wynken, Blynken, and Nod."

> Wynken, Blynken, and Nod one night
> Sailed off in a wooden shoe—
> Sailed on a river of crystal light,
> Into a sea of dew.

What makes "Wynken, Blynken, and Nod" a fantasy?

Ⓐ   Three men get in a boat.

Ⓑ   Three men sail in a wooden shoe.

Ⓒ   Three men sail to the sea.

5. Which picture name has the same ending sounds as the word in the box?

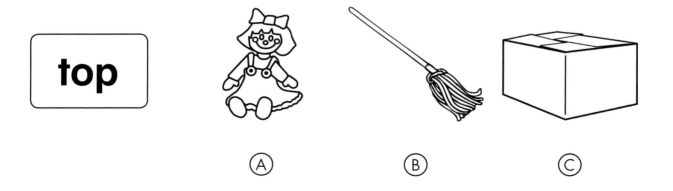

top

Ⓐ   Ⓑ   Ⓒ

6. Read the lines from the song "Wynken, Blynken, and Nod."

"We have come to fish for the herring fish
That live in this beautiful sea;
Nets of silver and gold have we!"
Said Wynken, Blynken, and Nod.

Who are the characters in the story?

(A) nets of silver and gold

(B) the beautiful sea

(C) Wynken, Blynken, and Nod

7. Read the lines from "On the Move."

It's the wind!
See how it makes the leaves
spin! spin! spin!

Which picture helps you know what the story is about?

(A)   (B)   (C)

8. Which sentence is correct?

Ⓐ The big cat.

Ⓑ Ran fast.

Ⓒ I am sad.

9. Read the lines from "On the Move."

In the park, I'm finding out
how some things can move about.
I stop to watch as things go by.
They float and fly up in the sky.

What could you ask to learn more about things that move in the park?

Ⓐ What is floating in the sky?

Ⓑ What color is the sky?

Ⓒ Where is the park?

10. Choose the words that go on the line.

A story must have a beginning, a middle, and _____.

a list   an animal   an end

Ⓐ   Ⓑ   Ⓒ

11. Read the lines from "On the Move."

> I see things move.
> Oh, *I* know!
> It's the wind!
> See how it makes the kites
> dance! dance! dance!

What might you picture in your mind?

Ⓐ   Ⓑ   Ⓒ

12. You are writing about your cat. Which idea is most interesting?

Ⓐ   I have a fat cat with spots.

Ⓑ   I have a cat.

Ⓒ   I pet my cat.

13. Which of these is a <u>wave</u>?

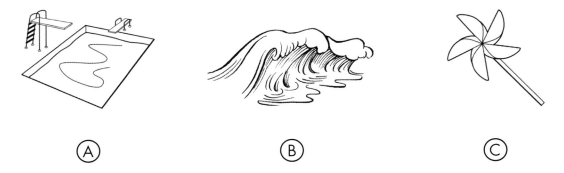

Ⓐ   Ⓑ   Ⓒ

14. What picture word has the same middle sound as the first picture word?

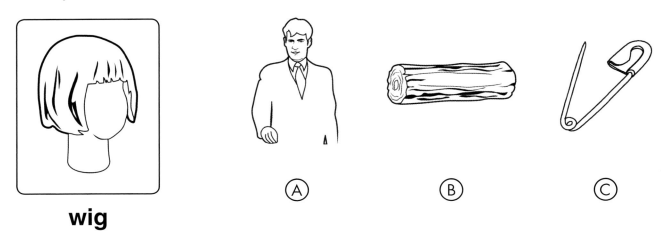

wig

Ⓐ   Ⓑ   Ⓒ

15. What end mark goes on the line?

> Can you feel the wind__

.   ?   !

Ⓐ   Ⓑ   Ⓒ

Student _____ Date _____

Student Theme Progress Test Record

Skills Tested	Item Numbers (cross out numbers for items answered incorrectly)	Student Score	Criterion Score	If the student scored less than the Criterion Score, use these Reteaching Tools:
Comprehension Create Images	1 7 11	_____ of 3	2 / 3	**Create Images:** Comprehension Bridge 3
Ask Questions	9	_____ of 1	1 / 1	**Ask Questions:** Comprehension Bridge 2
Target Skill Distinguish Fantasy from Reality	4	_____ of 1	1 / 1	**Distinguish Fantasy from Reality:** Teacher's Guide p. 92
Identify Character	6	_____ of 1	1 / 1	**Identify Character:** Teacher's Guide p. 86
Vocabulary	2 13	_____ of 2	1 / 2	**Vocabulary:** During independent reading time, review student's Vocabulary Journal and discuss how to improve the journal entries
Phonics *op, ot* Word Families	5	_____ of 1	1 / 1	***op, ot* Word Families:** Whole Class Charts p. 22 Teacher's Guide p. 74
Words with Short *i*	3 14	_____ of 2	1 / 2	**Words with Short *i*:** Whole Class Charts p. 27 Teacher's Guide p. 90
Writing: Process Writing Trait: Ideas	12	_____ of 1	1 / 1	**Trait: Ideas:** Writing Chart 7 Writing Bridge 5
Form: Story	10	_____ of 1	1 / 1	**Form: Story:** Writing Chart 8, 9 Writing Bridge 6
Writing: Grammar Complete Sentence: Ending Punctuation	15	_____ of 1	1 / 1	**Complete Sentence: Ending Punctuation:** Writing Resource Guide p. 5 Writer's Handbook pp. 8–9
Review Simple Sentence	8	_____ of 1	1 / 1	**Simple Sentence:** Writing Resource Guide p. 6 Writer's Handbook p. 6
		_____ / 15	12 / 15	

Answer Key

1. B   2. A   3. A   4. B   5. B   6. C   7. A   8. C   9. A   10. C

11. A   12. A   13. B   14. C   15. B

THEME ④ Ongoing Test Practice

Sample
Read the story. Fill in the circle next to your answer.

Animals Move

Cats run on four legs. Cats are fast! Birds run on two legs. They fly with two wings. Fish swim. A snake can move with no legs at all!

S. How do birds move?

Ⓐ   run on four legs

Ⓑ   fly with two wings

Ⓒ   swim

Fill in the circle next to your answer.

1. When will water <u>freeze</u>?

      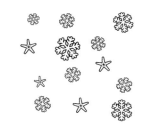

Ⓐ   Ⓑ   Ⓒ

2. Which picture name has the same ending sounds as **pin**?

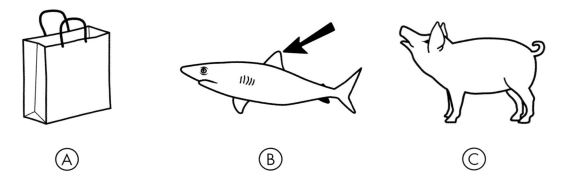

Ⓐ   Ⓑ   Ⓒ

> ### Kim's New Hat
> Kim has a new red hat. She put it on. She went out to play. Poor Kim. The wind blew her hat away!

3. What is important in the story?

Ⓐ   It is windy.

Ⓑ   The girl is Kim.

Ⓒ   The hat is red.

4. What happened to Kim's hat?

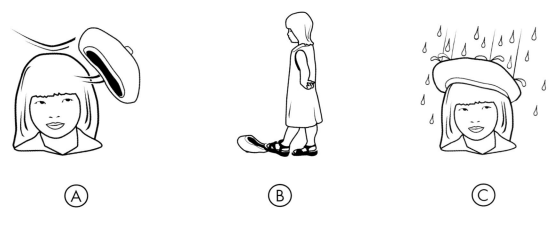

Ⓐ   Ⓑ   Ⓒ

THEME ④ Theme Progress Test

Fill in the circle next to your answer.

1. Which is a <u>liquid</u>?

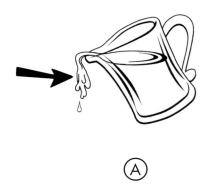      

   Ⓐ   Ⓑ   Ⓒ

2. Read the lines from the poem "I'm a Little Teapot."

> I'm a little teapot
> Short and stout.
> Here is my handle,
> Here is my spout.

What does a teapot have?

Ⓐ   a short lid

Ⓑ   a little cup

Ⓒ   a handle and a spout

3. Which picture word has the same middle sound as **tub**?

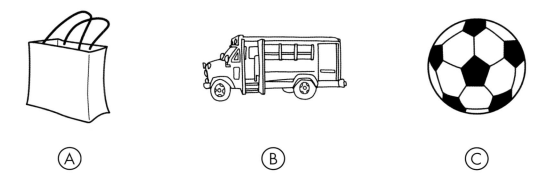

       Ⓐ   Ⓑ   Ⓒ

4. You want to write about rain. How should you begin?

    Ⓐ   Write about snow.

    Ⓑ   Write down ideas.

    Ⓒ   Draw a coat.

5. Read the lines from the poem "I'm a Little Teapot."

> When I get all steamed up,
> Hear me shout.
> Tip me over and pour me out!

What picture might you see in your mind?

       Ⓐ   Ⓑ   Ⓒ

6. Which sentence is correct?

    Ⓐ   Sam my name is.

    Ⓑ   My name is Sam.

    Ⓒ   My name Sam is.

7. Which picture name has the same ending sounds as the first picture?

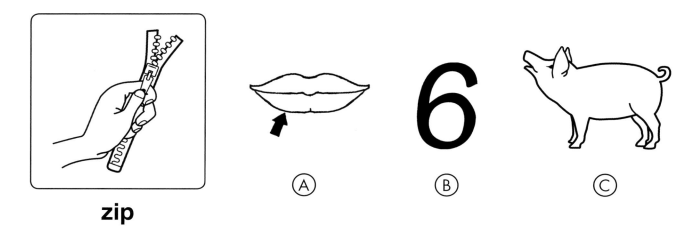

zip

          Ⓐ   Ⓑ   Ⓒ

8. What can you do to understand a story better?

    Ⓐ   Stop reading the story.

    Ⓑ   Write your own story.

    Ⓒ   Think about the important ideas in the story.

9. Which sentence is an asking sentence?

- Ⓐ Who is hot!

- Ⓑ It is hot.

- Ⓒ Why is it hot?

10. Which word rhymes with the picture word?

pan   win   nap

Ⓐ   Ⓑ   Ⓒ

11. What does the word <u>observe</u> mean?

I will <u>observe</u> the clouds in the sky.

- Ⓐ look at

- Ⓑ make up

- Ⓒ put down

12. Which mark goes at the end of the sentence?

The water is cold___

?

ⒶＡ

,

ⒷＢ

.

ⒸＣ

13. Read the lines from "Luisa's Lab."

> Ice doesn't fit the shape of the mug, either.
> Lily loves ice and wants to eat some!
> I learned that ice is a solid. It keeps its shape.

What is important to the story?

Ⓐ   Lily wants to eat ice.

Ⓑ   Ice is a solid.

Ⓒ   Lily loves ice.

14. What word would you use to start writing a story?

    Ⓐ   Then

    Ⓑ   Because

    Ⓒ   First

15. Which picture name has the same middle sound as **hug**?

    Ⓐ   Ⓑ   Ⓒ

THEME ④

Student Theme Progress Test Record

Skills Tested	Item Numbers (cross out numbers for items answered incorrectly)	Student Score	Criterion Score	If the student scored less than the Criterion Score, use these Reteaching Tools:
Comprehension Determine Importance	2 8 13	____ of 3	2 / 3	**Determine Importance:** Comprehension Bridge 4
Create Images	5	____ of 1	1 / 1	**Create Images:** Comprehension Bridge 3
Vocabulary	1 11	____ of 2	2 / 2	**Vocabulary:** During independent reading time, review student's Vocabulary Journal and discuss how to improve the journal entries
Phonics *ip, in* Word Families	7 10	____ of 2	1 / 2	*ip, in* **Word Families:** Whole Class Charts p. 31 Teacher's Guide p. 106
Words with Short *u*	3 15	____ of 2	1 / 2	**Words with Short *u*:** Whole Class Charts p. 36 Teacher's Guide p. 122
Writing: Process Writing Process: Prewriting	4	____ of 1	1 / 1	**Process: Prewriting:** Writing Chart 10 Writing Bridge 7
Organizational Pattern: Sequence	14	____ of 1	1 / 1	**Organizational Pattern: Sequence:** Writing Chart 11, 12 Writing Bridge 8
Writing: Grammar Telling Sentence	6 12	____ of 2	1 / 2	**Telling Sentence:** Writing Resource Guide p. 7 Writer's Handbook p. 5
Asking Sentence	9	____ of 1	1 / 1	**Asking Sentence:** Writing Resource Guide p. 8 Writer's Handbook p. 5
		____ / 15	11 / 15	

Answer Key

1. A   2. C   3. B   4. B   5. C   6. B   7. A   8. C   9. C   10. B

11. A   12. C   13. B   14. C   15. A

Name _____ Date _____

THEME ⑤ Ongoing Test Practice

Sample
Read the story. Fill in the circle next to your answer.

Kip at Bat

Kip put on his cap. Pop! He hit the ball. Up! Up! Where is it? Wendy got it. The ball is in her mitt.

S. Where are Kip and Wendy?

Ⓐ   Ⓑ   Ⓒ

Fill in the circle next to your answer.

1. What word has the same ending sounds as the picture word?

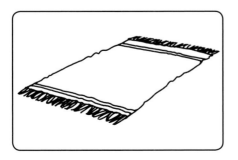

run   hug   nut

Ⓐ   Ⓑ   Ⓒ

2. Finish the sentence.

We have a picnic in the _____.

store

sky

park

(A)

(B)

(C)

A Bug Comes Inside

The bug ran in. It sat. "A rug is soft," it said.
Hop! "A bed is very soft."
Hop! "This is not soft. It is a box." The bug ran out.

---

3. Where was the bug?

(A)

(B)

(C)

4. Where did the bug hop first?

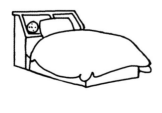

(A)

(B)

(C)

Name _____ Date _____

Fill in the circle next to your answer.

1. Which picture name rhymes with **fun**?

Ⓐ

Ⓑ

Ⓒ

2. Which of these is a <u>public</u> place?

Ⓐ

Ⓑ

Ⓒ

3. Choose the mark that goes at the end of the command.

Do not run into the street__

?

Ⓐ

,

Ⓑ

!

Ⓒ

4. Read the lines from "Outside My Window."

> Outside my window, I can see
> Houses, buildings, and a tree.

Which picture tells you where this takes place?

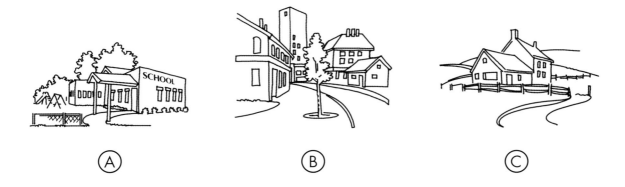

Ⓐ   Ⓑ   Ⓒ

5. Which picture name has the same middle sound as **met**?

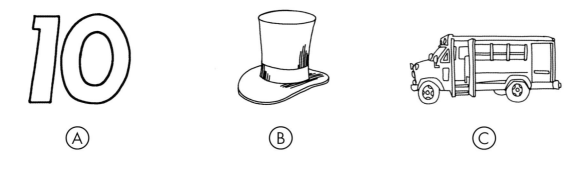

Ⓐ   Ⓑ   Ⓒ

6. Which of these is an asking sentence?

Ⓐ   Shut the door!

Ⓑ   What time is it?

Ⓒ   Timothy sat down.

7. Read the lines from "Shark in the Park."

> Timothy yells with all his might, "THERE'S A SHARK IN THE PARK!"
> A shark? Oh no! It's just a crow.

What is important in these lines?

(A) Timothy yells.

(B) Timothy did not see a shark.

(C) Timothy is in a park.

8. Which two words rhyme?

mug, mud	run, tug	mug, tug
(A)	(B)	(C)

9. You are going to write a story. What should you do after you have a story idea?

(A) Write with little letters.

(B) Write a draft.

(C) Write the ending.

10. Choose the word that belongs on the line.

   "Hello!" Ms. West calls to _____ the new child.

   (A) greet

   (B) playground

   (C) park

11. Read the lines from "Outside My Window."

   Children shouting far and near.
   Cars are beeping on the street.
   Music plays a steady beat.

   What is this place like?

   (A) Many animals live here.

   (B) The streets are empty.

   (C) There are many sounds.

12. Which sentence tells about a story?

(A) A story has a beginning, a middle, and an end.

(B) A story has no words.

(C) A story is a picture.

13. Read the lines from "Shark in the Park."

A shark?
Fancy that!
It's only a cat.

Which two words rhyme?

(A) shark, that

(B) that, cat

(C) shark, cat

14. Read the lines from "Outside My Window."

Outside my window, I call out.
"Hello out there! Hello!" I shout.
I call to children by their names.

What kind of child is this?

Ⓐ   quiet

Ⓑ   sleepy

Ⓒ   friendly

15. What word has the same middle sound as the picture word?

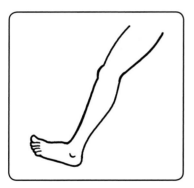

men   sit   hot
Ⓐ   Ⓑ   Ⓒ

Student _____ Date _____

THEME 5

Student Theme Progress Test Record

Skills Tested	Item Numbers (cross out numbers for items answered incorrectly)	Student Score	Criterion Score	If the student scored less than the Criterion Score, use these Reteaching Tools:
Comprehension Synthesize	4 11 14	_____ of 3	2 / 3	**Synthesize:** Comprehension Bridge 5
Determine Importance	7	_____ of 1	1 / 1	**Determine Importance:** Comprehension Bridge 4
Target Skill Recognize Rhythm and Rhyme	13	_____ of 1	1 / 1	**Recognize Rhythm and Rhyme:** Teacher's Guide p. 152
Vocabulary	2 10	_____ of 2	1 / 2	**Vocabulary:** During independent reading time, review student's Vocabulary Journal and discuss how to improve the journal entries
Phonics *un, ug* Word Families	1 8	_____ of 2	1 / 2	***un, ug* Word Families:** Whole Class Charts p. 40 Teacher's Guide p. 140
Words with Short *e*	5 15	_____ of 2	1 / 2	**Words with Short *e*:** Whole Class Charts p. 45 Teacher's Guide p. 156
Writing: Process Writing Form: Story	12	_____ of 1	1 / 1	**Form: Story:** Writing Chart 14, 15 Writing Bridge 10
Process: Drafting	9	_____ of 1	1 / 1	**Process: Drafting:** Writing Chart 13 Writing Bridge 9
Writing: Grammar Command/Express with End Punctuation	3	_____ of 1	1 / 1	**Command/Express with End Punctuation:** Writing Resource Guide p. 9 Writer's Handbook p. 5
Review Sentence Types	6	_____ of 1	1 / 1	**Sentence Types:** Writing Resource Guide p. 10 Writer's Handbook pp. 4–6
		_____ / 15	11 / 15	

Answer Key

1. B   2. A   3. C   4. B   5. A   6. B   7. B   8. C   9. B   10. A

11. C   12. A   13. B   14. C   15. A

THEME ⑥ Ongoing Test Practice

Sample
Read the story. Fill in the circle next to your answer.

At the Vet

Spot sits. The vet pets Spot. The vet looks. The vet says, "Spot is good."

S. What is Spot?

Ⓐ

Ⓑ

Ⓒ

Fill in the circle next to your answer.

I. What word has the same ending sounds as the picture word?

red
Ⓐ

wag
Ⓑ

web
Ⓒ

2. What does the word <u>deliver</u> mean?

He will <u>deliver</u> the box to my home.

take   open   hold

Ⓐ   Ⓑ   Ⓒ

Soccer Rules

Soccer is a fun game. But it has rules.
You must kick the ball. You cannot hit it. You must be quick. Go for the net. Play to win.
Soccer is fast. Go! Go! Go!

---

3. A soccer player must _____.

sit   run   hop

Ⓐ   Ⓑ   Ⓒ

4. What is needed to play soccer?

Ⓐ   Ⓑ   Ⓒ

Name _____ Date _____

THEME ⑥ Theme Progress Test

Fill in the circle next to your answer.

I. Which picture name rhymes with **pick**?

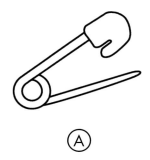

Ⓐ

Ⓑ

Ⓒ

2. Choose the word that belongs on the line.

The nurse _____ the doctor with her job.

Ⓐ   assists

Ⓑ   delivers

Ⓒ   worker

3. Read the sentences. Which sentence should be **last**?

Ⓐ   Then, Rick ate his lunch.

Ⓑ   First, Rick got some apples.

Ⓒ   Next, Rick got milk.

4. Read the lines from "What Do I Want to Be?"

> I'm a librarian. I help people find information they need for school or work.

Where does a librarian work?

(A)   in a zoo

(B)   on the street

(C)   in a library

5. Which picture name has the same ending sounds as **set**?

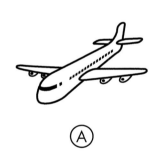      

(A)   (B)   (C)

6. Choose the word that belongs on the line.

The _____ can lick its paw.

(A)   red

(B)   cat

(C)   jump

7. Read this part of "Community Workers Protect Us."

> Firefighters protect our homes from danger.
> Ambulance drivers help sick people get to the hospital.

How are firefighters and ambulance drivers alike?

(A)   They both work in hospitals.

(B)   They both help people.

(C)   They both make food.

8. Which two words rhyme?

tack, back   tack, tick   back, bed

(A)   (B)   (C)

9. Choose the words that belong on the line.

The teacher's name is _____.

(A)   mrs. black

(B)   Mrs. black

(C)   Mrs. Black

10. Read the lines from "What Do I Want to Be?"

> How will I know the job for me?
> Who will I ask? Where will I go?
> All the people in town will know.

Who would be best to ask about a job?

(A) children playing

(B) people working

(C) people in cars

11. Read the story.

> A duck lives on a pond. It says "quack." The duck can swim.

What is a good detail to add to the story?

(A) The frog can hop.

(B) A tiger has big teeth.

(C) The duck can fly.

12. Read the lines from "What Do I Want to Be?"

> I'm a crossing guard. I help children cross the street safely.

Where does a crossing guard work?

Ⓐ near a school

Ⓑ at home

Ⓒ in a store

13. Which picture name rhymes with **pack**?

Ⓐ

Ⓑ

Ⓒ

14. Read the lines from "What Do I Want to Be?"

> Dr. Rubin: I'm a veterinarian.
> You can bring your pet to me for shots and check-ups.

Who does Dr. Rubin help?

Ⓐ

Ⓑ

Ⓒ

15. Which picture name rhymes with **bed**?

Ⓐ

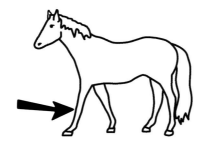
Ⓑ

Ⓒ

Student _____ Date _____

THEME 6

Student Theme Progress Test Record

Skills Tested	Item Numbers (cross out numbers for items answered incorrectly)	Student Score	Criterion Score	If the student scored less than the Criterion Score, use these Reteaching Tools:
Comprehension Infer	4 12 14	_____ of 3	2 / 3	**Infer:** Comprehension Bridge 6
Synthesize	7 10	_____ of 2	1 / 2	**Synthesize:** Comprehension Bridge 5
Vocabulary	2	_____ of 1	1 / 1	**Vocabulary:** During independent reading time, review student's Vocabulary Journal and discuss how to improve the journal entries
Phonics *et, ed* Word Families	5 15	_____ of 2	1 / 2	***et, ed* Word Families:** Whole Class Charts p. 49 Teacher's Guide p. 172
ick, ack Word Families	1 8 13	_____ of 3	2 / 3	***ick, ack* Word Families:** Whole Class Charts p. 54 Teacher's Guide p. 188
Writing: Process Writing Organizational Pattern: Main Idea and Details	11	_____ of 1	1 / 1	**Organizational Pattern: Main Idea and Details:** Writing Chart 17, 18 Writing Bridge 12
Trait: Organization	3	_____ of 1	1 / 1	**Trait: Organization:** Writing Chart 16 Writing Bridge 11
Writing: Grammar Naming Words: Animals and Things (common nouns)	6	_____ of 1	1 / 1	**Naming Words: Animals and Things (common nouns):** Writing Resource Guide p. 11 Writer's Handbook pp. 14–15
Naming Words: People and Places (proper nouns)	9	_____ of 1	1 / 1	**Naming Words: People and Places (proper nouns):** Writing Resource Guide p. 12 Writer's Handbook pp. 12–13
		_____ / 15	11 / 15	

Answer Key

1. B   2. A   3. A   4. C   5. A   6. B   7. B   8. A   9. C   10. B

11. C   12. A   13. B   14. C   15. A

Name _____ Date _____

THEME 7 Ongoing Test Practice

Sample

Read the story. Fill in the circle next to your answer.

How Plants Grow

Plants need three things. They need water. They need earth. They need light. Then plants can grow.

S. What should you do if you do not understand part of the story?

Ⓐ Circle letters.

Ⓑ Read the story again.

Ⓒ Cross out words.

Fill in the circle next to your answer.

I. Which picture shows <u>rainfall</u>?

Ⓐ   Ⓑ   Ⓒ

The Shell

Milly took a walk. Bump! Milly hit her toe.
"What is this?" Milly said. It was a shell.
Milly put it to her ear. Woosh! She heard the sea.

2. What did Milly hit her toe on?

   Ⓐ   a shell

   Ⓑ   the sea

   Ⓒ   a turtle

3. What should you do if you do not know what the word <u>woosh</u> means?

   Ⓐ   Spell the word.

   Ⓑ   Ask yourself questions.

   Ⓒ   Read a different story.

4. What shows you that Milly is talking?

.	?	" "
Ⓐ	Ⓑ	Ⓒ

Name _____ Date _____

Fill in the circle next to your answer.

I. Which picture name has the same beginning sound as **shed**?

Ⓐ

Ⓑ

Ⓒ

2. Read the lines from "The Bell in the Well."

> Suddenly, the sun began to shine.
> Jill slipped the bell into her pocket to keep it safe.
> By three o'clock, the laundry was dry.

What question could you ask if you don't understand these lines?

Ⓐ Is the sun shining today?

Ⓑ How did Jill get her name?

Ⓒ Why did Jill put the bell in her pocket?

3. Which two words rhyme?

fill, will   will, win   fell, fill

Ⓐ   Ⓑ   Ⓒ

4. Read the lines from "The Bell in the Well."

"I want it dry by three o'clock!"
Nasty Nell gave Jill impossible jobs
such as this all the time.

What do you do if you do not understand this?

Ⓐ   Find words that rhyme.

Ⓑ   Ask yourself questions.

Ⓒ   Spell each word.

5. Which word goes on the line?

My dog _____ runs outdoors.

SHeP   shep   Shep

Ⓐ   Ⓑ   Ⓒ

6. Read the lines from "The Bell in the Well."

> Jolly Molly invited Jill to stay and live with them. From that day on, every day felt like a sunny day.

What do these lines mean?

Ⓐ   Everyone felt hot.

Ⓑ   Everyone felt happy.

Ⓒ   Everyone felt sad.

7. Read the sentences.

> "It is cold!" Mom said. "Get your mittens."

What shows you that Mom is talking?

!

Ⓐ

" "

Ⓑ

.

Ⓒ

8. Which picture name has the same ending sounds as **tell**?

Ⓐ

Ⓑ

Ⓒ

9. Read the lines from "Billy Bear."

> "When will it be fall?"
> Mom says, "Very soon, my dear.
> In not too long at all."

What makes this a poem?

Ⓐ It has words that rhyme.

Ⓑ Characters talk.

Ⓒ There is a mom in it.

10. Read the lines from "The Bell in the Well."

> Nasty Nell sent Jill to get firewood.
> "Fill three sacks!" she yelled.
> It was impossible.
> The fog was too thick.

Why couldn't Jill get firewood?

Ⓐ She couldn't see it.

Ⓑ She didn't have a sack.

Ⓒ She didn't know what it was.

11. Read the lines from "Billy Bear."

> In winter, Billy Bear's too cold.
> "When will it be spring?"

When is it too cold for Billy Bear?

Ⓐ never

Ⓑ in the spring

Ⓒ in the winter

12. Read the lines from "The Bell in the Well."

> Around and around we go,
> As the wind gently blows.
> Our friendship grows and grows
> Beneath the sun's warm glow.

Which words show that the writer likes sunshine?

Ⓐ our friendship grows

Ⓑ the wind gently blows

Ⓒ the sun's warm glow

13. Which word goes on the line?

Snow fell on _____.

thursday   Thursday   thursDay
Ⓐ   Ⓑ   Ⓒ

14. Choose the word that goes on the line.

There are 365 days in a _____.

thermometer   drop   year
Ⓐ   Ⓑ   Ⓒ

15. Read the lines from "The Bell in the Well."

Jill hung out the laundry and the rain began to fall.
"This will never dry by three!" she cried. "Whatever
shall I do?"

What is Jill's problem?

Ⓐ   The laundry won't dry in time.

Ⓑ   She doesn't like to do laundry.

Ⓒ   She is cold in the rain.

Student _____ Date _____

Student Theme Progress Test Record

Skills Tested	Item Numbers (cross out numbers for items answered incorrectly)	Student Score	Criterion Score	If the student scored less than the Criterion Score, use these Reteaching Tools:
Comprehension Monitor Understanding	2 4 11	_____ of 3	2 / 3	**Monitor Understanding:** Comprehension Bridge 7
Infer	6 10	_____ of 2	1 / 2	**Infer:** Comprehension Bridge 6
Target Skill Identify Plot	15	_____ of 1	1 / 1	**Identify Plot:** Teacher's Guide p. 224
Understand Dialogue	7	_____ of 1	1 / 1	**Understand Dialogue:** Teacher's Guide p. 218
Vocabulary	14	_____ of 1	1 / 1	**Vocabulary:** During independent reading time, review student's Vocabulary Journal and discuss how to improve the journal entries
Phonics *th, sh* Digraphs	1	_____ of 1	1 / 1	***th, sh* Digraphs:** Whole Class Charts p. 58 Teacher's Guide p. 206
ill, ell Word Families	3 8	_____ of 2	1 / 2	***ill, ell* Word Families:** Whole Class Charts p. 63 Teacher's Guide p. 222
Writing: Process Writing Form: Poem	9	_____ of 1	1 / 1	**Form: Poem:** Writing Chart 20, 21 Writing Bridge 14
Trait: Voice	12	_____ of 1	1 / 1	**Trait: Voice:** Writing Chart 19 Writing Bridge 13
Writing: Grammar Naming Words: Days, Months, Holidays	13	_____ of 1	1 / 1	**Naming Words: Days, Months, Holidays:** Writing Resource Guide p. 13 Writer's Handbook p. 13
Naming Words: Names and Titles	5	_____ of 1	1 / 1	**Naming Words: Names and Titles:** Writing Resource Guide p. 14 Writer's Handbook pp. 11–13
		_____ / 15	12 / 15	

Answer Key

1. B	2. C	3. A	4. B	5. C	6. B	7. B	8. A	9. A	10. A
11. C	12. C	13. B	14. C	15. A					

THEME ⑧ Ongoing Test Practice

Sample
Read the story. Fill in the circle next to your answer.

What Is a Lake?

A lake is made of water. It has land on all sides. Some lakes are big. Some lakes are small. Lakes are home for many animals. Fish, frogs, and turtles all live in or around lakes.

S. How can you tell what the word <u>turtles</u> means?

   Ⓐ Read the story title.

   Ⓑ Spell the word.

   Ⓒ Read other sentences.

Fill in the circle next to your answer.

1. What word has the same ending sounds as the picture word?

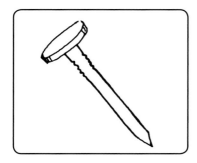

   pail   sad   nose
    Ⓐ   Ⓑ   Ⓒ

    Ongoing Test Practice

What Is a River?

Water in a river moves. It can go to a lake. A river has fresh water. It does not have salt in it. There is land on the sides. This land is the <u>bank</u>. People fish from the sides.

2. You get stuck on the word <u>fresh</u>. What should you do?

   Ⓐ   Spell the word.

   Ⓑ   Read on. Think about what makes sense.

   Ⓒ   Stop reading.

3. In this story, <u>bank</u> means _____.

   Ⓐ   a box where a child keeps coins

   Ⓑ   the land on the sides of a river

   Ⓒ   a building that keeps money

4. What would be a good detail to add to this story?

   Ⓐ   Some lakes are salty.

   Ⓑ   Fish is good for lunch.

   Ⓒ   Many fish live in a river.

THEME 8 Theme Progress Test

Fill in the circle next to your answer.

1. Which picture name has the same ending sounds as **rake**?

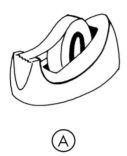  

Ⓐ   Ⓑ   Ⓒ

2. Read the lines from "Over the River."

> The horse knows the way to carry the sleigh,
> Through the white and drifted snow.

How can you tell what the word <u>sleigh</u> means?

Ⓐ   Look at the picture.

Ⓑ   Read the lines out loud.

Ⓒ   Find a word that rhymes.

3. Choose the word that goes on the line.

It is hot in _____.

July   july   jump

  Ⓐ   Ⓑ   Ⓒ

4. Choose the word that goes on the line.

It is a cold day. The _____ is low.

cloud   temperature   mistake

  Ⓐ   Ⓑ   Ⓒ

5. Read the lines. What could you add to the story?

> Dell puts on a warm jacket and a hat.
> He goes out to play.

Ⓐ   Dell likes summertime.

Ⓑ   Dell puts on his red mittens.

Ⓒ   Dell wears shorts.

6. Which picture name has the same ending sounds as **hail**?

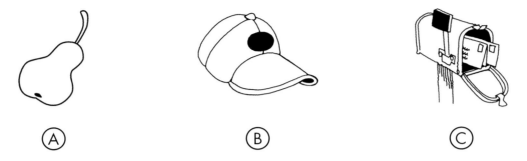

  Ⓐ   Ⓑ   Ⓒ

7. Which word goes on the line?

 Gail has two red _____.

 hats   hat   Hat

 Ⓐ   Ⓑ   Ⓒ

8. Read the lines from "How Should I Dress?"

> A raincoat is a great choice for a rainy day.
> Rain boots and hats will also help keep you dry.

You are stuck on the word <u>raincoat</u>. What should you do?

 Ⓐ Break the word into two small words.

 Ⓑ Skip over the word.

 Ⓒ Spell the word.

9. Which two words rhyme?

pan, pain   main, pain   main, make

Ⓐ   Ⓑ   Ⓒ

10. Read the lines from "How Should I Dress?"

> Wait a minute, there's a storm today.
> You should stay inside to play!

What should you do if you do not understand part of the story?

Ⓐ   Cross out words.

Ⓑ   Read the story again.

Ⓒ   Circle the capital letters.

11. Which two words rhyme?

mail, make   take, tale   make, take

Ⓐ   Ⓑ   Ⓒ

12. Read the lines from "Over the River."

> Over the river and through the wood,
> To Grandfather's house we go.

You get stuck on the word <u>Grandfather's</u>. What should you do?

(A) Stop reading.

(B) Break the word into parts.

(C) Spell the word.

13. Read the lines from "How Should I Dress?"

> A hat will keep your head
> warm on a snowy day.
> Mittens and a coat are also
> great for sledding in the snow.

What more could you add to these lines?

(A) A swimsuit is good for swimming.

(B) Boots will keep your feet warm.

(C) Shorts can help you stay cool.

14. What two words rhyme?

     tale, sale   got, gale   bill, tell

       Ⓐ   Ⓑ   Ⓒ

15. Read the lines from "Over the River."

> Oh, how the wind does blow!
> It stings the toes and bites the nose,
> As over the ground we go.

What stings the toes?

Ⓐ   the nose

Ⓑ   the ground

Ⓒ   the wind

THEME 8

Student Theme Progress Test Record

Skills Tested	Item Numbers (cross out numbers for items answered incorrectly)	Student Score	Criterion Score	If the student scored less than the Criterion Score, use these Reteaching Tools:
Comprehension Use Fix-Up Strategies	2 8 12	____ of 3	2 / 3	**Use Fix-Up Strategies:** Comprehension Bridge 8
Monitor Understanding	10 15	____ of 2	1 / 2	**Monitor Understanding:** Comprehension Bridge 7
Vocabulary	4	____ of 1	1 / 1	**Vocabulary:** During independent reading time, review student's Vocabulary Journal and discuss how to improve the journal entries
Phonics *ake, ale* Word Families	1 11 14	____ of 3	2 / 3	***ake, ale* Word Families:** Whole Class Charts p. 67 Teacher's Guide p. 238
ail, ain Word Families	6 9	____ of 2	1 / 2	***ail, ain* Word Families:** Whole Class Charts p. 72 Teacher's Guide p. 254
Writing: Process Writing Organizational Pattern: Main Idea and Details	13	____ of 1	1 / 1	**Organizational Pattern: Main Idea and Details:** Writing Chart 23, 24 Writing Bridge 16
Process: Revising	5	____ of 1	1 / 1	**Process: Revising:** Writing Chart 22 Writing Bridge 15
Writing: Grammar Review All Naming Words	3	____ of 1	1 / 1	**Naming Words:** Writing Resource Guide p. 15 Writer's Handbook pp. 12–15
Naming Words: One or More (Singular/Plural)	7	____ of 1	1 / 1	**Naming Words: One or More (Singular/Plural):** Writing Resource Guide p. 16 Writer's Handbook p. 15
		____ / 15	11 / 15	

Answer Key

1. C	2. A	3. A	4. B	5. B	6. C	7. A	8. A	9. B	10. B

11. C	12. B	13. B	14. A	15. C

Name _____ Date _____

Fill in the circle next to your answer.

1. Which picture name has the same beginning sound as **shell**?

Ⓐ   Ⓑ   Ⓒ

2. Which two words rhyme?

mail, sail   mug, sag   mop, mold

Ⓐ   Ⓑ   Ⓒ

3. Read the poem.

Jack, Jack,
What is in your sack?
Wet, wet,
A little wet pet!

Which two words rhyme?

Jack, what   little, wet   wet, pet

Ⓐ   Ⓑ   Ⓒ

Read the story. Fill in the circle next to your answer.

The Lion and the Mouse

Lion lay in the grass. He was asleep. Mouse ran on top of Lion. Lion woke up. He opened his mouth to eat Mouse.

Mouse said, "Wait! Maybe one day I can help you."

Lion laughed. He asked, "How can a little mouse help a big lion?" But he let Mouse go.

One day, a man got Lion. He tied Lion up.

Mouse saw Lion. He ran over. Mouse bit the rope. Lion got away.

"You see," said Mouse. "I am little, but I can help."

Mouse and Lion became friends.

4. How was Mouse a good friend?

(A)   He ran on top of Lion.

(B)   He helped Lion.

(C)   He tied Lion up.

5. Which picture shows where the story takes place?

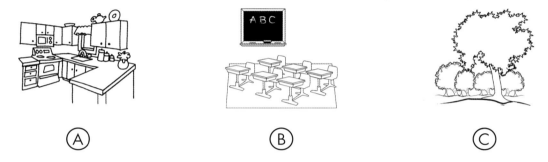

(A)   (B)   (C)

6. What makes "The Lion and the Mouse" make-believe?

(A)   Animals talk.

(B)   A lion sleeps.

(C)   A mouse runs.

7. Read the line from "The Lion and the Mouse."

Mouse said, "Wait! Maybe one day I can help you."

What shows you that Mouse is talking?

(A)   (B)   (C)

Read the story. Fill in the circle next to your answer.

How to Make a Postcard

You will need:

heavy white paper

scissors

ruler

crayons

pencil

stamp

1. Make a box on the paper. Make it 6 inches on one side. Make it 4 inches on the other side. Cut the box out. This is the postcard.

2. Think of a place you like. Make a picture of it on the card.

3. Turn the card over. First make a line down the middle. Next go to the left side. Write a letter to a <u>friend</u>. Then go to the right side. Put an address there.

4. Put a stamp in the corner. Mail the card.

8. You get stuck on the sentence <u>Put a stamp in the corner</u>. What picture helps you understand?

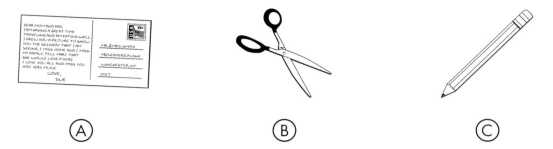

Ⓐ Ⓑ Ⓒ

9. What question can you ask if you don't understand Step 3?

Ⓐ Where do I live?

Ⓑ Why do I need to draw a line?

Ⓒ What picture can I draw?

10. In Step 3, what word shows you what to start with?

middle   next   first

Ⓐ Ⓑ Ⓒ

11. What does the word <u>friend</u> mean?

Ⓐ your favorite plant

Ⓑ someone you get along with

Ⓒ someone you do not know

Read the story. Fill in the circle next to your answer.

The Lost Pass

"Oh, no!" said Ling. "I cannot <u>locate</u> my pass."

"When did you see it?" asked Dad.

Ling said, "Mom gave it to me. Now I cannot find it!"

Dad said, "Where was the first place you put it?"

"I put it with my bag," said Ling.

"Look in your bag," said Dad.

It was not there.

"What did you do next?" asked Dad.

"I put on my coat," said Ling.

"Look in your coat," said Dad.

Ling looked in the pocket.
She found it!

12. How will Ling use her pass?

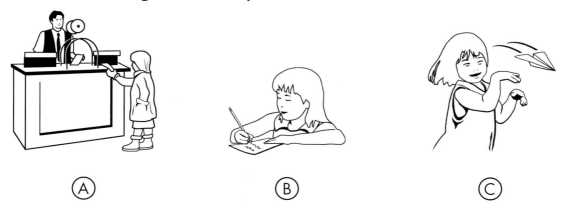

Ⓐ   Ⓑ   Ⓒ

13. What is the weather like in the story?

warm   hot   cold

Ⓐ   Ⓑ   Ⓒ

14. What does the word <u>locate</u> mean?

Ⓐ   find

Ⓑ   read

Ⓒ   color

15. Who is "The Lost Pass" mostly about?

Mom   Dad   Ling

Ⓐ   Ⓑ   Ⓒ

Read the story. Fill in the circle next to your answer.

Helping Earth

Earth is our home. We must take care of it.

We could cut down too many trees. Then animals would not have homes. We would not have any more wood. Wood is used to make houses.

We could use up all the water. Then plants would be dry. Animals would not have enough to drink. We would not have enough water.

You can help. Use less water. Be <u>aware</u> of how much water you use. Turn it off when you are done.

Use old boxes. Recycle cans and bottles. To recycle is to use again.

---

16. What can you ask to learn more about how to save water?

   Ⓐ   Would you like a glass of water?

   Ⓑ   What can I do to use less water?

   Ⓒ   How much water is in the ocean?

17. Which idea is most important to the story?

    Ⓐ   Wood is used to make houses.

    Ⓑ   Use old boxes.

    Ⓒ   We must take care of Earth.

18. What does it mean to be <u>aware</u>?

to pay attention   to be kind   to drink more
     Ⓐ   Ⓑ   Ⓒ

19. What word has the same middle sound as the picture word?

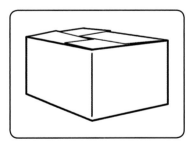

      tip   top   tap
      Ⓐ   Ⓑ   Ⓒ

20. Which picture word has the same middle sound as **cut**?

    Ⓐ   Ⓑ   Ⓒ

MID-YEAR REVIEW

Mid-Year Review Test Record

Comprehension		Cross out numbers for items answered incorrectly.	
Make Connections	4	Synthesize	13
Ask Questions	16	Infer	12
Create Images	5	Monitor Understanding	9
Determine Importance	17	Use Fix-Up Strategies	8

If student has difficulty with Comprehension, use the Comprehension Bridges. **Total Comprehension Score** _____ / 8

Target Skill			
Distinguish Fantasy from Reality	6	Identify Character	15
Understand Dialogue	7	Recognize Rhythm and Rhyme	3

If student has difficulty with Target Skills, use the Teacher's Guide lessons. **Total Target Skill Score** _____ / 4

Vocabulary			
	11 14 18		

If student has difficulty with Vocabulary, review student's Vocabulary Journal. **Total Vocabulary Score** _____ / 3

Phonics			
Words with Short *o*	19	*ail, ain* Word Families	2
th, sh Digraphs	1	Words with Short *u*	20

If student has difficulty with Phonics, use the Whole Class Charts and Teacher's Guide lessons. **Total Phonics Score** _____ / 4

Writing: Process Writing			
Organizational Pattern: Sequence	10		

If student has difficulty with Writing, use the Writing Bridges. **Total Writing: Process Writing Score** _____ / 1

Total Score _____ / 20

Answer Key

1. C	2. A	3. C	4. B	5. C	6. A	7. B	8. A	9. B	10. C
11. B	12. A	13. C	14. A	15. C	16. B	17. C	18. A	19. B	20. A

Name _____ Date _____

THEME 9 Ongoing Test Practice

Sample
Read the story. Fill in the circle next to your answer.

At the Park

Tran went to the park. He fed the ducks. He saw a toad. Tran went home. He fed his pet fish. He made his bed. Tran was happy.

S. How were the park and home alike?

Ⓐ Tran fed animals.

Ⓑ Tran made beds.

Ⓒ Tran saw toads.

Fill in the circle next to your answer.

I. What word has the same ending sounds as the picture word?

rake   road   hope

Ⓐ   Ⓑ   Ⓒ

2. Choose the word that goes on the line.

Bud says, "That is a good _____!"

game
Ⓐ

cake
Ⓑ

scent
Ⓒ

The Best Clothes

It is a cold day. What clothes should you wear? Warm clothes are best. It is a good day to wear a hat. It is a good day to wear mittens. Do not forget your coat!

It is a hot day. What clothes should you wear? Cool clothes are best. It is a good day to wear a hat and shorts.

---

3. What clothes are used only on a cold day?

Ⓐ

Ⓑ

Ⓒ

4. What could you wear on both a hot day and a cold day?

a hat
Ⓐ

a swimsuit
Ⓑ

a coat
Ⓒ

Name _____ Date _____

Fill in the circle next to your answer.

1. Which picture name has the same ending sounds as **told**?

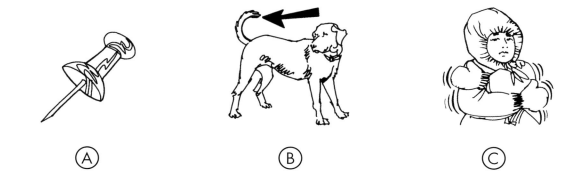

Ⓐ   Ⓑ   Ⓒ

2. Read the lines from "Fox, Beware!"

> There are soft-colored days when the birds are nesting. The fox lies still in a new-found lair. But out of the quiet grows a grumbling rumble.

How are the birds and the fox alike?

Ⓐ   They both can fly.

Ⓑ   They are both in their homes.

Ⓒ   They both live in a lair.

3. Choose the word that goes on the line.

Hope _____ a ball. It goes over a fence.

kicks   kicking   will kick

Ⓐ   Ⓑ   Ⓒ

4. Choose the word that goes on the line.

I will hide. Can you _____ me?

peaceful   find   depend

Ⓐ   Ⓑ   Ⓒ

5. Read the lines from "Fox, Beware!"

> There are blazing days in the burst of summer.
> The fox stays cool in a deep dark lair.
> But the beautiful trees are troubled and trembling.

It is hot outside. How is it different where the fox is?

Ⓐ   It is bright.

Ⓑ   It is cool.

Ⓒ   It is loud.

6. Which picture word has the same ending sounds as the word **poke**?

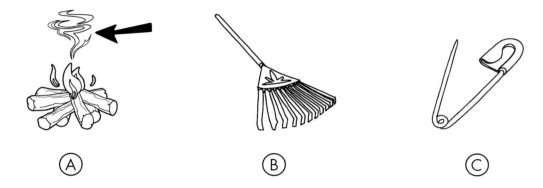

(A)   (B)   (C)

7. Read the sentence. It has a mistake in it.

| the fox made a nice home under a tree. |

Which sentence below is correct?

(A)   The fox made a nice home under a tree.

(B)   the Fox made a nice home under a tree.

(C)   the fox made a nice home under a tree?

8. Which two words rhyme?

road, rail   toad, tad   road, toad

(A)   (B)   (C)

9. Read the lines from "The Sky." Look at the picture.

The wind whips around
To boldly bully the bees.
But I dance in it all—
Just the sky and me.

What does the picture help you see?

Ⓐ   The girl sees a dark cloud in the sky.

Ⓑ   The girl is sad.

Ⓒ   The girl likes being outdoors.

10. Read the lines from "Fox, Beware!"

Cars race and roar on the slick new surface.
Hurry now, fox.
You can't stay there!

Which words have the same beginning sound?

race, roar   hurry, fox   cars, race

Ⓐ   Ⓑ   Ⓒ

11. Read the lines from "The Sky."

> Raindrops drizzle down
> On the flowers and weeds.
> Sun smiles from above
> On the beautiful trees.

How are the flowers and weeds alike?

Ⓐ They are both trees.

Ⓑ They are both smiling.

Ⓒ They are both wet from rain.

12. Read the story.

> Darren wants to play baseball with his friends. He puts on his cap. But Darren doesn't have a baseball glove!

What could you add to the story to fix Darren's problem?

Ⓐ Darren takes off his cap.

Ⓑ Darren can use his brother's old glove.

Ⓒ Darren can't play baseball.

13. Which two words rhyme?

cope, cape

hope, cope

hope, hop

(A)

(B)

(C)

14. Read the line from "Fox, Beware!"

> The woodcutters' saws are screeching and tearing.

You get stuck on the word <u>woodcutters'</u>. What should you do?

(A) Break the word into parts.

(B) Spell the word.

(C) Stop reading.

15. Which word goes on the line?

Mr. Hale burned the food. He _____ it too long.

cook

cooking

cooked

(A)

(B)

(C)

Student _____ Date _____

THEME 9

Student Theme Progress Test Record

Skills Tested	Item Numbers (cross out numbers for items answered incorrectly)	Student Score	Criterion Score	If the student scored less than the Criterion Score, use these Reteaching Tools:
Comprehension Make Connections: Compare and Contrast Information	2 5 11	_____ of 3	2 / 3	**Make Connections: Compare and Contrast Information:** Comprehension Bridge 9
Use Fix-Up Strategies	9 14	_____ of 2	1 / 2	**Use Fix-Up Strategies:** Comprehension Bridge 8
Target Skill Recognize Alliteration	10	_____ of 1	1 / 1	**Recognize Alliteration:** Teacher's Guide p. 284
Vocabulary	4	_____ of 1	1 / 1	**Vocabulary:** During independent reading time, review student's Vocabulary Journal and discuss how to improve the journal entries
Phonics *oke, ope* Word Families	6 13	_____ of 2	1 / 2	***oke, ope* Word Families:** Whole Class Charts p. 76 Teacher's Guide p. 272
oad, old Word Families	1 8	_____ of 2	1 / 2	***oad, old* Word Families:** Whole Class Charts p. 81 Teacher's Guide p. 288
Writing: Process Writing Organizational Pattern: Problem and Solution	12	_____ of 1	1 / 1	**Organizational Pattern: Problem and Solution:** Writing Chart 26, 27 Writing Bridge 18
Process: Editing	7	_____ of 1	1 / 1	**Process: Editing:** Writing Chart 25 Writing Bridge 17
Writing: Grammar Action Words That Tell About Now (Present Tense)	3	_____ of 1	1 / 1	**Action Words That Tell About Now (Present Tense):** Writing Resource Guide p. 17 Writer's Handbook p. 15
Action Words That Tell About the Past (Past Tense)	15	_____ of 1	1 / 1	**Action Words That Tell About the Past (Past Tense):** Writing Resource Guide p. 18 Writer's Handbook p. 15
		_____ / 15	11 / 15	

Answer Key

1. C   2. B   3. A   4. B   5. B   6. A   7. A   8. C   9. C   10. A

11. C   12. B   13. B   14. A   15. C

THEME ⑩ Ongoing Test Practice

Sample
Read the story. Fill in the circle next to your answer.

Ana's New Room

Ana moved to a new house. She got her own room.
Ana put a light by her bed. She put a rug on the floor.
She put her toys in a box. Having her own room was fun!

S. What else could Ana put in her room?

Ⓐ   Ⓑ   Ⓒ

Fill in the circle next to your answer.

I. Which picture shows a <u>mountain</u>?

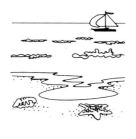      

Ⓐ   Ⓑ   Ⓒ

2. Which two words rhyme?

ride, sight   night, nail   night, sight

Ⓐ   Ⓑ   Ⓒ

Look Up!

"I see a big bear," said Mike.

"Oh, no! Where?" asked Luis.

"Look up!" said Mike. "I see a fox!"

"Where?" asked Luis.

"Look at the white one. See the fluffy part," said Mike.

"Oh! I see a goat and a monkey," said Luis. "This is fun."

---

3. What are the boys in the story looking at?

Ⓐ   Ⓑ   Ⓒ

---

4. Where could the boys see a real monkey?

a post office   a zoo   a grocery store

Ⓐ   Ⓑ   Ⓒ

7. Which two words rhyme?

right, rig   right, might   might, mold

Ⓐ   Ⓑ   Ⓒ

8. Which sentence uses the best describing words?

Ⓐ   The cats run around.

Ⓑ   Two yellow cats race around the tall tree.

Ⓒ   Two cats walk around the yard.

9. Read the lines from "My Adventure with Fluffy."

> The Pacific Ocean is the largest ocean in the world.
> It covers about one third of Earth!

How is the Pacific Ocean different from other oceans?

Ⓐ   It is larger.

Ⓑ   It is smaller.

Ⓒ   It is colder.

10. Read the line from "My Adventure with Fluffy."

> Fluffy and I looked for cacti and animals while we were in the desert.

What question could you ask to learn more about the desert?

Ⓐ   What kinds of animals live in the desert?

Ⓑ   How do you spell the word <u>desert</u>?

Ⓒ   How long was Fluffy in the desert?

11. Read the line from "Yellowstone National Park."

> Old Faithful is a geyser that sprays hot water into the air.

What is a geyser?

Ⓐ   a kind of rain

Ⓑ   a place to swim

Ⓒ   hot water from the ground

12. Which word has the same ending sounds as the picture word?

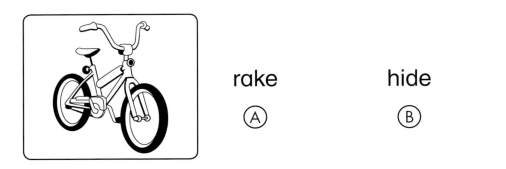

rake   hide   hike

(A)   (B)   (C)

13. Read the lines from "My Adventure with Fluffy."

> We also visited Mount Baldy.
> During the winter, it is covered with snow.
> Fluffy and I love to play in snow!

What is the weather like on Mount Baldy?

(A)   warm

(B)   hot

(C)   cold

14. This is Mike. What word rhymes with the name **Mike**?

like   lake   met

Ⓐ   Ⓑ   Ⓒ

15. Read the lines from "My Adventure with Fluffy."

> Next we went to Sequoia National Park.
> The sequoia trees there are the largest trees
> in the world.

How are sequoia trees different from other trees?

Ⓐ   They are smaller.

Ⓑ   They are bigger.

Ⓒ   They are greener.

THEME 10

Student Theme Progress Test Record

Skills Tested	Item Numbers (cross out numbers for items answered incorrectly)	Student Score	Criterion Score	If the student scored less than the Criterion Score, use these Reteaching Tools:
Comprehension Ask Questions: Meaning	10 11 13	_____ of 3	2 / 3	**Ask Questions: Meaning:** Comprehension Bridge 10
Make Connections: Compare and Contrast Information	9 15	_____ of 2	1 / 2	**Make Connections: Compare and Contrast Information:** Comprehension Bridge 9
Vocabulary	5	_____ of 1	1 / 1	**Vocabulary:** During independent reading time, review student's Vocabulary Journal and discuss how to improve the journal entries
Phonics *ike, ide* Word Families	1 12 14	_____ of 3	2 / 3	***ike, ide* Word Families:** Whole Class Charts p. 85 Teacher's Guide p. 304
ie, ight Word Families	3 7	_____ of 2	1 / 2	***ie, ight* Word Families:** Whole Class Charts p. 90 Teacher's Guide p. 320
Writing: Process Writing Form: Personal Narrative	2	_____ of 1	1 / 1	**Form: Personal Narrative:** Writing Chart 29, 30 Writing Bridge 20
Trait: Word Choice	8	_____ of 1	1 / 1	**Trait: Word Choice:** Writing Chart 28 Writing Bridge 19
Writing: Grammar Review Action Words (Verbs)	4	_____ of 1	1 / 1	**Action Words (Verbs):** Writing Resource Guide p. 19 Writer's Handbook pp. 15–16
Subject-Verb Agreement	6	_____ of 1	1 / 1	**Subject-Verb Agreement:** Writing Resource Guide p. 20 Writer's Handbook p. 5
		_____ / 15	11 / 15	

Answer Key

1. A   2. A   3. C   4. A   5. B   6. C   7. B   8. B   9. A   10. A

11. C   12. C   13. C   14. A   15. B

Name _____ Date _____

Sample
Fill in the circle next to your answer.

Sarah's Birthday

It is Sarah's birthday. She has a birthday cake. Her family sings "Happy Birthday" to her.

S. What picture helps you know what the story is about?

(A)　　　　　　　(B)　　　　　　　(C)

Fill in the circle next to your answer.

1. What word has the same middle sound as the picture word?

mule

cute　　　　mother　　　　rug

(A)　　　　　(B)　　　　　(C)

The Big Tree

The big tree was very tall. He spoke to a young tree. "You must grow tall, like me. It is your job to grow tall. You will make a nice home for birds and small <u>mammals</u>. You can give them food. This is what trees do."

2. What picture helps you know what the story is about?

Ⓐ   Ⓑ   Ⓒ

3. Which of these is a <u>mammal</u>?

house   tree   squirrel

Ⓐ   Ⓑ   Ⓒ

4. You are the young tree. What do you hear?

Ⓐ   Ⓑ   Ⓒ

Name _____ Date _____

THEME **11** Theme Progress Test

Fill in the circle next to your answer.

I. Which picture name has the same middle sound as **tune**?

Ⓐ

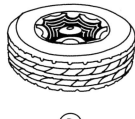

Ⓑ

Ⓒ

2. What does the word <u>occurs</u> mean?

Your birthday <u>occurs</u> once a year.

Ⓐ moves

Ⓑ happens

Ⓒ changes

3. Choose the word that goes on the line.

The ducklings hatched. _____ began to peep.

She   It   They

Ⓐ   Ⓑ   Ⓒ

4. Read the lines from "What a Duck!"

One spring morning, the ducklings hatched.
One, two, three, four, five little peeps.

Which picture tells you about the story?

Ⓐ

Ⓑ

Ⓒ

5. Which two words rhyme?

seam, seed

Ⓐ

seed, feed

Ⓑ

need, eat

Ⓒ

6. What helps you see a story better when you read it?

Ⓐ small words

Ⓑ pictures in your mind

Ⓒ page numbers

7. Read the sentences. The sentences are numbered.

> (I) Three frogs move to a new pond. (2) Baby Frog gets lost. (3) The other frogs find him.

Which sentence is the **end** of the story?

Ⓐ   sentence I

Ⓑ   sentence 2

Ⓒ   sentence 3

8. Which two words rhyme?

ten, bed   bead, boy   team, beam

Ⓐ   Ⓑ   Ⓒ

9. How would you start a letter to your grandma?

Ⓐ   Dear Grandma,

Ⓑ   See you soon!

Ⓒ   Bye Grandma,

10. Read the lines from "Over in the Meadow."

> Over in the meadow,
> In the sand in the sun,
> Lived an old mother toadie.

Where does this poem take place?

(A) a house

(B) a meadow

(C) a toad

11. Read the lines from "What a Duck!"

> Mother Duck came back to her nest and proudly looked at her eggs. It was time to wait.

What can you ask to learn more about Mother Duck and her eggs?

(A) Is it raining?

(B) Can Mother Duck swim?

(C) How long will Mother Duck have to wait?

12. Which of these is a <u>reptile</u>?

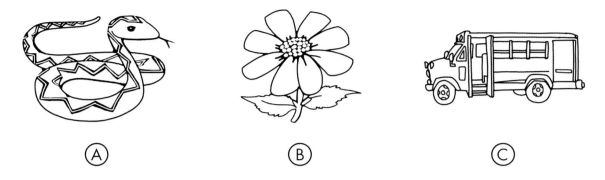

   Ⓐ   Ⓑ   Ⓒ

13. Read the sentences. They are numbered.

> (1) Alex went to the zoo. (2) Alex saw a tiger. (3) Alex saw a monkey. (4) Alex saw an elephant.

How can you make the sentences better?

   Ⓐ   use different animals

   Ⓑ   add the connecting words First, Then, Next

   Ⓒ   use periods to end the sentences

14. Read the lines from "Over in the Meadow."

> So they winked and they blinked
> In the sand in the sun.

What place do you picture in your mind?

Ⓐ   Ⓑ   Ⓒ

15. Which word goes on the line?

Sam _____ to read each day.

wanting   wants   want

Ⓐ   Ⓑ   Ⓒ

Student _____   Date _____

Student Theme Progress Test Record

Skills Tested	Item Numbers (cross out numbers for items answered incorrectly)	Student Score	Criterion Score	If the student scored less than the Criterion Score, use these Reteaching Tools:
Comprehension Create Images: Enhance Understanding	4 6 14	_____ of 3	2 / 3	**Create Images: Enhance Understanding:** Comprehension Bridge 11
Ask Questions: Meaning	11	_____ of 1	1 / 1	**Ask Questions: Meaning:** Comprehension Bridge 10
Target Skill Identify Story Structure	7	_____ of 1	1 / 1	**Identify Story Structure:** Teacher's Guide p. 356
Identify Setting	10	_____ of 1	1 / 1	**Identify Setting:** Teacher's Guide p. 350
Vocabulary	2 12	_____ of 2	1 / 2	**Vocabulary:** During independent reading time, review student's Vocabulary Journal and discuss how to improve the journal entries
Phonics *eed, eam* Word Families	5 8	_____ of 2	1 / 2	***eed, eam* Word Families:** Whole Class Charts p. 94 Teacher's Guide p. 338
Words with Long *u*	1	_____ of 1	1 / 1	**Words with Long *u*:** Whole Class Charts p. 99 Teacher's Guide p. 354
Writing: **Process Writing** Trait: Sentence Fluency	13	_____ of 1	1 / 1	**Trait: Sentence Fluency:** Writing Chart 31 Writing Bridge 21
Form: Letter	9	_____ of 1	1 / 1	**Form: Letter:** Writing Chart 32, 33 Writing Bridge 22
Writing: Grammar Subject-Verb Agreement	15	_____ of 1	1 / 1	**Subject-Verb Agreement:** Writing Resource Guide p. 20 Writer's Handbook p. 5
Subject Pronouns	3	_____ of 1	1 / 1	**Subject Pronouns:** Writing Resource Guide p. 22 Writer's Handbook p. 17
		_____ / 15	12 / 15	

Answer Key

1. C	2. B	3. C	4. A	5. B	6. B	7. C	8. C	9. A	10. B

11. C   12. A   13. B   14. A   15. B

THEME ⑫ Ongoing Test Practice

Sample
Fill in the circle next to your answer.

A Bat

A bat flew out of a cave. It saw a bug. The bat ate the bug.

S. What is the story mostly about?

Ⓐ a rock

Ⓑ a bat

Ⓒ a cave

Fill in the circle next to your answer.

I. Which picture shows <u>roots</u>?

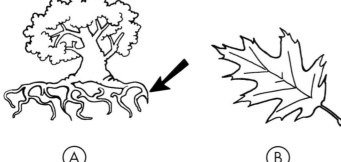

Ⓐ   Ⓑ   Ⓒ

Janet's Butterfly Poem

Janet likes to write. Janet writes a poem. It is about a butterfly. The butterfly lives in a garden. The butterfly flies with its friends. They land on flowers.

Janet is finished with her poem. She reads it to her mom.

2. What is the main idea of this story?

    Ⓐ A girl reads to her mom.

    Ⓑ A girl writes a poem.

    Ⓒ A girl plants a garden.

3. What is Janet's poem mostly about?

    Ⓐ what a butterfly does

    Ⓑ flying with friends

    Ⓒ where butterflies live

4. Which word is made of two smaller words?

flowers	garden	butterfly
Ⓐ	Ⓑ	Ⓒ

Name _____ Date _____

THEME (12) Theme Progress Test

Read each question. Fill in the circle for the correct answer.

1. Which picture name has the same beginning sounds as the first picture?

 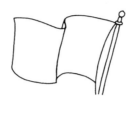  

               Ⓐ   Ⓑ   Ⓒ

2. | Kendra and her dad like flowers. They planted seeds in a pot. They watered the seeds. Then they put the pot in a sunny window. |

What did Kendra and her dad do **last**?

Ⓐ   They watered the seeds.

Ⓑ   They planted the seeds.

Ⓒ   They put the pot in a window.

3. You write a story. How could you share your story with others?

   Ⓐ   Change the name of the story.

   Ⓑ   Write another story.

   Ⓒ   Read the story out loud.

4. Read the lines from the poem "Other Lands."

> Up into the cherry tree
> Who did climb but little me?
> I held the tree with both my hands
> And looked across in other lands.

Which picture helps you know what the poem is about?

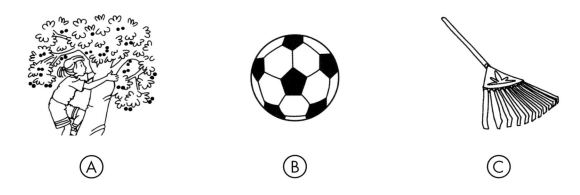

     Ⓐ   Ⓑ   Ⓒ

5. Which word is made of two smaller words?

    picnic   morning   ladybug

     Ⓐ   Ⓑ   Ⓒ

6. Who is the author of the book?

(A) bugs

(B) Tim Totter

(C) Lupe

7. Which word belongs on the line?

Malik likes Mom. Malik hugs _____.

she
(A)

her
(B)

it
(C)

8. Which two smaller words are used to make the picture word?

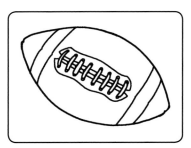

(A) foot + ball

(B) foot + shoe

(C) toe + ball

9. Choose the word that belongs on the line.

_____ are young plants.

Ⓐ Growth

Ⓑ Seedlings

Ⓒ Roots

10. Which picture name has the same beginning sounds as **blue**?

Ⓐ   Ⓑ   Ⓒ

11. Choose the word that belongs on the line.

Mario planted all the flowers.
He _____ quickly!

growth   cycle   finished

Ⓐ   Ⓑ   Ⓒ

12. Read the lines from "How to Grow a Sunflower."

> In autumn, when the sunflowers have finished flowering, cut off the flower heads. Store them in a cool, dry place for a few weeks.
> Collect the seeds by shaking the dry flower heads into a bag.

What is this story mostly about?

Ⓐ finding cool, dry places

Ⓑ growing flowers

Ⓒ collecting sunflower seeds

13. Look at the picture.

Which word belongs on the line?

_____ are at school.

He   It   They

Ⓐ   Ⓑ   Ⓒ

14. Read the lines from "Other Lands."

> If I could find a higher tree
> Farther and farther I could see,
> Past the roads on either side
> And onward into the world so wide.

What is the poem mostly about?

Ⓐ   seeing new places

Ⓑ   driving on roads

Ⓒ   running far

15. Read this part of "How to Grow a Hyacinth."

> Start growing your hyacinth in autumn. Fill the bottom part of the jar with water. Place the bulb in the top of the jar.

What is the story mostly about?

Ⓐ   things to do in autumn

Ⓑ   growing a hyacinth

Ⓒ   how to fill a jar

Student _____   Date _____

THEME 12

Student Theme Progress Test Record

Skills Tested	Item Numbers (cross out numbers for items answered incorrectly)	Student Score	Criterion Score	If the student scored less than the Criterion Score, use these Reteaching Tools:
Comprehension Determine Importance: Main Idea	12 14 15	_____ of 3	2 / 3	**Determine Importance: Main Idea:** Comprehension Bridge 12
Create Images: Enhance Understanding	4	_____ of 1	1 / 1	**Create Images: Enhance Understanding:** Comprehension Bridge 11
Target Skill Locate Author and Illustrator	6	_____ of 1	1 / 1	**Locate Author and Illustrator:** Teacher's Guide p. 382
Vocabulary	9 11	_____ of 2	1 / 2	**Vocabulary:** During Independent Reading time, review student's Vocabulary Journal and discuss how to improve the journal entries
Phonics Consonant *l* Blends	1 10	_____ of 2	1 / 2	**Consonant *l* Blends:** Whole Class Chart p. 103 Teacher's Guide p. 370
Compound Words	5 8	_____ of 2	1 / 2	**Compound Words:** Whole Class Chart p. 108 Teacher's Guide p. 386
Writing: Process Writing Process: Publishing	3	_____ of 1	1 / 1	**Process: Publishing:** Writing Chart 34 Writing Bridge 23
Form: Procedural Text	2	_____ of 1	1 / 1	**Form: Procedural Text:** Writing Chart 35, 36 Writing Bridge 24
Writing: Grammar Object Pronouns	7	_____ of 1	1 / 1	**Object Pronouns:** Writing Resource Guide p. 23 Writer's Handbook p. 17
Review Pronouns	13	_____ of 1	1 / 1	**Pronouns:** Writing Resource Guide p. 24 Writer's Handbook p. 17
		_____ / 15	11 / 15	

Answer Key

1. A   2. C   3. C   4. A   5. C   6. B   7. B   8. A   9. B   10. B

11. C   12. C   13. C   14. A   15. B

THEME 13 Ongoing Test Practice

Sample
Read the story. Fill in the circle next to your answer.

Lisa's Garden

Lisa and her dad went to the store. They got the things that they needed. They planted seeds in a pot. They watered them. They put the pot in a sunny window.

The flowers grew! "What a pretty garden!" Lisa said.

S. What is one thing Lisa needs from the store?

   Ⓐ   Ⓑ   Ⓒ

Fill in the circle next to your answer.

1. Glen plays the drums very well. He has _____.

     song   talent   time

      Ⓐ   Ⓑ   Ⓒ

Pikas

A pika is a small mountain animal. It looks a bit like a rabbit. But it does not have long ears. Pikas are short and round. In summer, they eat some grass. They cut even more grass. They make a pile of it. They let it dry. Then they hide it. When winter comes, pikas eat the stored grass.

2. What do pikas eat?

rabbits
(A)

pile
(B)

grass
(C)

3. What did the author of this story do?

(A) wrote the story

(B) drew the pictures

(C) acted it out

4. When do pikas eat the stored grass?

summer
(A)

spring
(B)

winter
(C)

THEME 13 Theme Progress Test

Fill in the circle next to your answer.

I. Which picture name has the same middle sound as **shirt**?

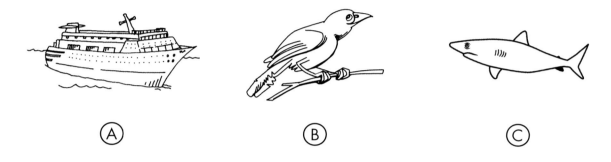

    Ⓐ   Ⓑ   Ⓒ

2. Read the lines from "A Play for All."

> Bart wasn't sure about the play.
> "I'd rather just watch," said Bart.
> Ms. Fry said, "That's fine.
> You may watch the play
> and join in when you're ready."

What is something important to retell?

Ⓐ   Bart was in the play.

Ⓑ   Ms. Fry watched the play.

Ⓒ   Bart wanted to watch the play.

3. What word has the same ending sound as the picture word?

cry

crack
Ⓐ

fly
Ⓑ

car
Ⓒ

4. Look at the picture. Which word belongs on the line?

The clerk has a _____ bag.

Ⓐ sweet

Ⓑ little

Ⓒ torn

5. What word has the same ending sound as the word in the box?

dry

sky
Ⓐ

you
Ⓑ

red
Ⓒ

6. Choose the word that goes on the line.

Lori found a dollar. She smiled. She felt _____.

    fast   tall   happy

    Ⓐ   Ⓑ   Ⓒ

7. What does the word <u>individual</u> mean?

This small juice box is made for an <u>individual</u>.

Ⓐ   one person

Ⓑ   three people

Ⓒ   family

8. What is the first step in prewriting?

Ⓐ   Check spelling.

Ⓑ   Read out loud.

Ⓒ   Find an idea.

9. Read the lines from "I'm Special, You're Special."

> I'm good at that,
> You're good at this.
> When we work together,
> We just can't miss!

What is this poem mostly about?

Ⓐ working together

Ⓑ missing something

Ⓒ being good

10. Read the lines from "A Play for All."

> Bart jumped up and said, "This play is great!
> I should do my part."
> "I'm glad you chose to join in, Bart," said Ms. Fry.

What does Bart do?

Ⓐ He jumps rope.

Ⓑ He joins the play.

Ⓒ He sits quietly.

11. Which picture name has the same middle sound as **cord**?

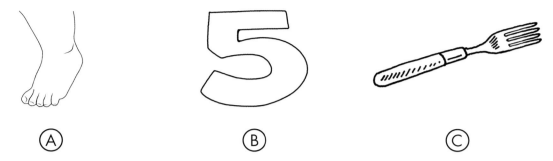

(A)   (B)   (C)

12. Read the lines.

> It is hot! Joella and her family go to the pool. But Joella can't swim. She sits and watches. Swimming looks fun.

What could you write to fix Joella's problem?

(A)   Joella goes home and reads a book.

(B)   Joella asks her mom to teach her to swim.

(C)   Joella has a cold drink.

13. What does the illustrator of a story do?

(A)   writes the story

(B)   reads the story out loud

(C)   draws the pictures

14. Read the lines from "I'm Special, You're Special."

> On a warm, spring day,
> We're clearing a lot
> For a place to play.

What is happening in this poem?

Ⓐ   They are making a place to play.

Ⓑ   It is sunny and warm.

Ⓒ   They are playing a new game.

15. Read the lines from "A Play for All."

> We wrote a play about what we had learned.
> Everyone in the class had a part in the play.

What is this story mainly about?

Ⓐ   going to class

Ⓑ   playing together

Ⓒ   writing a class play

Student _____ Date _____

THEME 13

Student Theme Progress Test Record

Skills Tested	Item Numbers (cross out numbers for items answered incorrectly)	Student Score	Criterion Score	If the student scored less than the Criterion Score, use these Reteaching Tools:
Comprehension Synthesize: Retell	2 10 14	_____ of 3	2 / 3	**Synthesize: Retell:** Comprehension Bridge 13
Determine Importance: Main Idea	9 15	_____ of 2	1 / 2	**Determine Importance: Main Idea:** Comprehension Bridge 12
Target Skill Understand Role of Author and Illustrator	13	_____ of 1	1 / 1	**Understand Role of Author and Illustrator:** Teacher's Guide p. 416
Vocabulary	7	_____ of 1	1 / 1	**Vocabulary:** During independent reading time, review student's Vocabulary Journal and discuss how to improve the journal entries
Phonics r-Controlled Vowels	1 11	_____ of 2	1 / 2	**r-Controlled Vowels:** Whole Class Charts p. 112 Teacher's Guide p. 404
Words with -y	3 5	_____ of 2	1 / 2	**Words with -y:** Whole Class Charts p. 117 Teacher's Guide p. 420
Writing: Process Writing Organizational Pattern: Problem and Solution	12	_____ of 1	1 / 1	**Organizational Pattern: Problem and Solution:** Writing Chart 38, 39 Writing Bridge 26
Process: Prewriting	8	_____ of 1	1 / 1	**Process: Prewriting:** Writing Chart 37 Writing Bridge 25
Writing: Grammar Describing Words (Adjectives): Color and Size	4	_____ of 1	1 / 1	**Describing Words (Adjectives):** **Color and Size:** Writing Resource Guide p. 25 Writer's Handbook p. 18
Describing Words (Adjectives): Feelings	6	_____ of 1	1 / 1	**Describing Words (Adjectives): Feelings:** Writing Resource Guide p. 26 Writer's Handbook p. 18
		_____ / 15	11 / 15	

Answer Key

1. B   2. C   3. B   4. B   5. A   6. C   7. A   8. C   9. A   10. B

11. C   12. B   13. C   14. A   15. C

THEME ⑭ Ongoing Test Practice

Sample
Read the story. Fill in the circle next to your answer.

Two Kinds of Buses

There are two kinds of buses. There are school buses. There are city buses. School buses take children to school. Anyone can ride a city bus. A city bus can take you all over the city.

S. Where would you find people of many different ages?

   Ⓐ   city bus

   Ⓑ   school bus

   Ⓒ   first grade

Fill in the circle next to your answer.

I. Which picture name has the same beginning sounds as **pride**?

Ⓐ

Ⓑ

Ⓒ

2. What does the word <u>knowledge</u> mean?

Theo reads a lot. He has <u>knowledge</u> about many things.

what you feel   a book   what you learn

Ⓐ   Ⓑ   Ⓒ

Green Grass

"Look out the window. Snow! I do not want to see snow!" said Lee. "When will things be green?"

Grace made a surprise for Lee. She asked Lee to look out the window. Lee smiled, "I said I wanted to see green grass. So you painted some on the window!"

---

3. Choose the word that goes on the line.

Lee does not like _____.

green   grass   winter

Ⓐ   Ⓑ   Ⓒ

4. How does Lee feel at the end of the story?

happy   mad   sad

Ⓐ   Ⓑ   Ⓒ

Name _____ Date _____

THEME 14 Theme Progress Test

Fill in the circle next to your answer.

1. Which picture name has the same beginning sounds as **trap**?

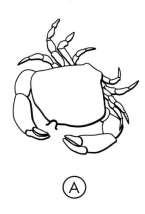

Ⓐ

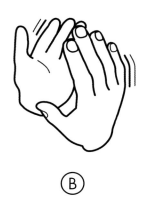

Ⓑ

Ⓒ

2. Read the lines from "Citizens To Look Up To."

One day George Washington asked Betsy to sew a flag for the United States. Betsy got right to work.

Which picture shows something Betsy was good at?

Ⓐ

Ⓑ

Ⓒ

3. What word has the same beginning sounds as the picture word?

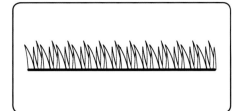

green   fast   bring

   Ⓐ   Ⓑ   Ⓒ

4. Read the sentence. It has a mistake.

grapes are a good snack.

Which new sentence is correct?

Ⓐ   Grapes are a good snack

Ⓑ   Grapes are a good snack.

Ⓒ   grapes are a good snack

5. What word has the same beginning sounds as the picture word?

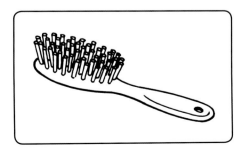

great   cab   breeze

   Ⓐ   Ⓑ   Ⓒ

6. Choose the word that goes on the line.

Beto took a bite of corn. It tasted _____.

sweet   sad   red

(A)   (B)   (C)

7. Choose the word that goes on the line.

The game must be played with _____.
Everyone gets a turn.

(A)   promise

(B)   fairness

(C)   loyalty

8. Choose the words that go on the line.

A report has _____.

(A)   facts about people and things

(B)   many jokes

(C)   make-believe places

9. Read the lines from "Make New Friends."

> A circle is round,
> it has no end.
> That's how long
> I will be your friend.

How long will the people in the song be friends?

(A) one year

(B) always

(C) a few days

10. Read the lines from "Citizens To Look Up To."

> When Alejandra grew up, she found out that some
> adults never went to school and didn't learn to read.
> Alejandra wanted to help, so she volunteered to teach
> adults how to read.

What is an important detail to retell from these lines?

(A) Alejandra went to school.

(B) Alejandra grew up.

(C) Alejandra teaches reading.

11. Which word has the same beginning sounds as **prize**?

back

(A)

press

(B)

globe

(C)

12. Choose the word that goes on the line.

Mandy was cooking. She put _____ eggs in a bowl.

jump

(A)

milk

(B)

some

(C)

13. Read the lines from "Make New Friends."

Make new friends,
but keep the old.
One is silver,
the other is gold.

What is something important to retell from the lines?

(A) Keep your old friends.

(B) One friend is silver.

(C) Gold is a nice color.

14. Read the sentence from "Citizens To Look Up To."

> Martin Luther King, Jr., gave speeches and worked hard to make sure all people had the same rights.

Why did Martin Luther King, Jr., give speeches?

Ⓐ   He wanted lots of people to hear his ideas.

Ⓑ   He did not like to sit down.

Ⓒ   He did not want anyone to hear him.

15. Which picture name has the same beginning sounds as **brick**?

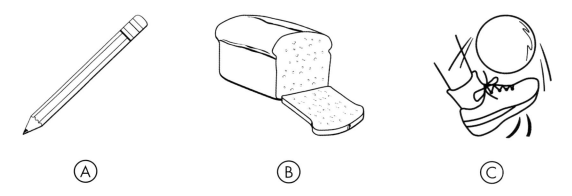

Ⓐ   Ⓑ   Ⓒ

Student _____ Date _____

Student Theme Progress Test Record

Skills Tested	Item Numbers (cross out numbers for items answered incorrectly)	Student Score	Criterion Score	If the student scored less than the Criterion Score, use these Reteaching Tools:
Comprehension Infer: Conclusions	2 9 14	_____ of 3	2 / 3	**Infer: Conclusions:** Comprehension Bridge 14
Synthesize: Retell	10 13	_____ of 2	1 / 2	**Synthesize: Retell:** Comprehension Bridge 13
Vocabulary	7	_____ of 1	1 / 1	**Vocabulary:** During independent reading time, review student's Vocabulary Journal and discuss how to improve the journal entries
Phonics *gr, tr* Blends	1 3	_____ of 2	1 / 2	***gr, tr* Blends** Whole Class Charts p. 121 Teacher's Guide p. 436
br, pr Blends	5 11 15	_____ of 3	2 / 3	***br, pr* Blends** Whole Class Charts p. 126 Teacher's Guide p. 452
Writing: Process Writing Form: Report	8	_____ of 1	1 / 1	**Form: Report:** Writing Chart 41, 42 Writing Bridge 28
Trait: Conventions	4	_____ of 1	1 / 1	**Trait: Conventions:** Writing Chart 40 Writing Bridge 27
Writing: Grammar Describing Words (Adjectives): Senses	6	_____ of 1	1 / 1	**Describing Words (Adjectives): Senses:** Writing Resource Guide p. 27 Writer's Handbook p. 18
Describing Words (Adjectives): How Many	12	_____ of 1	1 / 1	**Describing Words (Adjectives): How Many:** Writing Resource Guide p. 28 Writer's Handbook p. 18
		_____ / 15	11 / 15	

Answer Key

1. C   2. B   3. A   4. B   5. C   6. A   7. B   8. A   9. B   10. C

11. B   12. C   13. A   14. A   15. B

THEME (15) Ongoing Test Practice

Sample
Read the story. Fill in the circle next to your answer.

Skunk!

Animals need a way to stay safe. Deer can run fast. Bears and lions are strong. A skunk has a bad smell. It uses its smell to stay safe from other animals.

S. How does a skunk stay safe?

   (A) It can run fast.

   (B) It makes a bad smell.

   (C) It is strong.

Fill in the circle next to your answer.

I. Which word begins with the same sounds as the picture word?

   stop   jar   runs
   (A)   (B)   (C)

A New Animal

"What kind of fish is that?" Mia asked. "You are not a fish!" she said to the animal. "You have a tail and small legs, but you live in the water. What *are* you?" She came back each day. The animal seemed to change each day. One day she knew what the animal was. It was a frog!

2. Why did Mia think the animal was a fish?

It had legs.   It was a frog.   It was in water.

Ⓐ   Ⓑ   Ⓒ

3. What means the same as <u>habitat</u>?

Frogs live in a wet <u>habitat</u>.

living place   big book   tall building

Ⓐ   Ⓑ   Ⓒ

4. What did the animal look like when Mia first saw it?

Ⓐ   Ⓑ   Ⓒ

Name _____   Date _____

Fill in the circle next to your answer.

I. Which word sounds like what it means?

dance   hiss   train

Ⓐ   Ⓑ   Ⓒ

2. What word begins with the same sounds as the picture word?

stay   smile   skip

Ⓐ   Ⓑ   Ⓒ

3. Read the lines from "The Underground Dance."

> It's me. I'm a miner with a drill and a light,
> working down deep where it's dark as night.

Why does the miner need a light?

Ⓐ   He works with animals.

Ⓑ   He works indoors.

Ⓒ   He works underground.

4. Choose the word that goes on the line.

The mole dug a _____ in the dirt.

tunnel
Ⓐ

creatures
Ⓑ

ground
Ⓒ

5. What can you do to make your writing look good?

Ⓐ   Use all capital letters.

Ⓑ   Write with neat and clear letters.

Ⓒ   Cross out words.

6. Which picture word begins with the same sounds as **swim**?

Ⓐ

Ⓑ

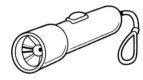

Ⓒ

7. What should you do if you do not understand what you read?

Ⓐ   Read a different book.

Ⓑ   Put the book down.

Ⓒ   Read the book again.

8. Look at the picture. Which word goes on the line?

Sam pets the _____ cat.

    soft   dog   run

    Ⓐ   Ⓑ   Ⓒ

9. Read the story.

> Ron did not hear the bell on his clock. He got out of bed. He saw the bus drive by.

What could you write to tell Ron's problem?

Ⓐ   Ron did not have a clock.

Ⓑ   Ron missed the bus.

Ⓒ   Ron was sick.

10. Read the lines from "Robin Needs a Home."

> First, Robin spots a lovely hole.
> She climbs inside but finds a mole.
> Mole says, "This home is mine, not yours."
>
> Next, into a cave she flies,
> But finds a bear of giant size.
> Bear says, "This home is mine, not yours."

Why does the author use the words, "This home is mine, not yours" many times?

Ⓐ   to tell that the homes are not for Robin

Ⓑ   to make each line rhyme

Ⓒ   to show what Robin says to the animals

11. Which of these is a <u>creature</u>?

Ⓐ

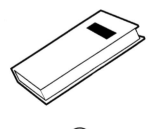
Ⓑ

Ⓒ

12. Which sentence is correct?

   Ⓐ Is frog and a toad.

   Ⓑ Jump a frog can.

   Ⓒ A frog can swim.

13. Read the lines from "The Underground Dance."

> It's me. I'm a centipede with lots of legs, digging in the earth to lay my eggs.

What is true about a centipede?

   Ⓐ It has two legs.

   Ⓑ It lays eggs in the dirt.

   Ⓒ It never digs.

14. What word begins with the same sounds as the picture word?

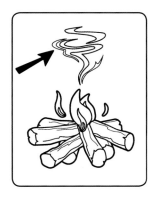

       smog   stack   skid

        Ⓐ   Ⓑ   Ⓒ

15. Read the lines from "Robin Needs a Home."

Robin then flies through a door,
And wakes a boy from sleep mid-snore.
Boy says, "This home is mine, not yours."

So where will tired Robin rest?
Finally, she finds a nest.

Where does Robin find a bed of her own?

Ⓐ   in a house

Ⓑ   in a boy's bed

Ⓒ   in a bird's nest

Student _____ Date _____

Student Theme Progress Test Record

Skills Tested	Item Numbers (cross out numbers for items answered incorrectly)	Student Score	Criterion Score	If the student scored less than the Criterion Score, use these Reteaching Tools:
Comprehension Monitor Understanding: Reread Text	3 7 15	____ of 3	2 / 3	**Monitor Understanding: Reread Text:** Comprehension Bridge 15
Infer: Conclusions	13	____ of 1	1 / 1	**Infer: Conclusions:** Comprehension Bridge 14
Target Skill Identify Repetition of Language	10	____ of 1	1 / 1	**Identify Repetition of Language:** Teacher's Guide p. 482
Recognize Onomatopoeia	1	____ of 1	1 / 1	**Recognize Onomatopoeia:** Teacher's Guide p. 488
Vocabulary	4 11	____ of 2	1 / 2	**Vocabulary:** During independent reading time, review student's Vocabulary Journal and discuss how to improve the journal entries
Phonics *st, sk* Blends	2	____ of 1	1 / 1	***st, sk* Blends:** Whole Class Charts p. 130 Teacher's Guide p. 470
sw, sm Blends	6 14	____ of 2	1 / 2	***sw, sm* Blends:** Whole Class Charts p. 135 Teacher's Guide p. 486
Writing: Process Writing Trait: Presentation	5	____ of 1	1 / 1	**Trait: Presentation:** Writing Chart 43 Writing Bridge 29
Form: Story	9	____ of 1	1 / 1	**Form: Story:** Writing Chart 44, 45 Writing Bridge 30
Writing: Grammar Review Adjectives	8	____ of 1	1 / 1	**Adjectives:** Writing Resource Guide p. 29 Writer's Handbook p. 18
Review Simple Sentences	12	____ of 1	1 / 1	**Simple Sentences:** Writing Resource Guide p. 30 Writer's Handbook p. 6
		____ / 15	12 / 15	

Answer Key

1. B   2. A   3. C   4. A   5. B   6. B   7. C   8. A   9. B   10. A

11. C   12. C   13. B   14. A   15. C

Name _____   Date _____

THEME ⑯ Ongoing Test Practice

Sample
Read the story. Fill in the circle next to your answer.

Liam's Catch

Liam caught a butterfly.

"Liam," said Fiona, "you must let the butterfly go."

"You're right," Liam said. He opened his hands and watched the butterfly fly away.

S. What is a <u>butterfly</u>?

  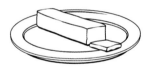

Ⓐ   Ⓑ   Ⓒ

Fill in the circle next to your answer.

I. What word has the same ending sounds as the picture word?

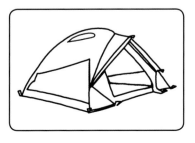

pond   spent   camp
Ⓐ   Ⓑ   Ⓒ

Moth or Butterfly?

A moth is not the same as a butterfly. A moth flies at night. A butterfly flies during the daytime.

A moth has a fat body. Its body has short hair. A butterfly has a thin body. It does not have hairs.

When a moth lands, its wings spread out flat. When a butterfly lands, it keeps its wings up high.

Now you know the difference between a moth and a butterfly.

2. You get stuck on the word <u>difference</u>. How can you break up the word to sound it out?

di fferen ce
Ⓐ

dif fer ence
Ⓑ

d iffe re nce
Ⓒ

3. What <u>feature</u> does a moth have?

wings
Ⓐ

fins
Ⓑ

shell
Ⓒ

4. You do not know the word <u>daytime</u>. How can you break up the word to sound it out?

d aytime
Ⓐ

da yt ime
Ⓑ

day time
Ⓒ

Name _____ Date _____

THEME 16 Theme Progress Test

Fill in the circle next to your answer.

1. Read the line from "Amazing Animals."

> If you had the trunk of an elephant or the wings of an albatross, what could you do?

You do not know the word <u>elephant</u>. What can help you read the word?

Ⓐ   Break the word into parts.

Ⓑ   Read the word <u>wings</u>.

Ⓒ   Look at the table of contents.

2. Who is showing <u>balance</u>?

Ⓐ   Ⓑ   Ⓒ

3. What word begins with the same sound as the picture word?

champ   bath   coach

Ⓐ   Ⓑ   Ⓒ

4. Which sentence is correct?

Ⓐ Bark a dog can.

Ⓑ Cats four legs.

Ⓒ Birds can fly.

5. Which picture name has the same ending sounds as **hand**?

Ⓐ   Ⓑ   Ⓒ

6. Read this part of "Amazing Animals."

> The long wings of an albatross allow it to glide through the air without needing to flap its wings.

You do not know the word <u>albatross</u>. How would you break it apart?

a lbat ross   al ba tross   al batro ss
   Ⓐ   Ⓑ   Ⓒ

7. What should you do when you edit your writing?

Ⓐ Check for capital letters.

Ⓑ Think of ideas for writing.

Ⓒ Color a picture.

8. Which word ends with the same sounds as **best**?

ten   nest   story
Ⓐ   Ⓑ   Ⓒ

9. How can you join these two sentences?

> Papa bird looks for food. Mama bird sits with the babies.

  Ⓐ Papa bird looks for food Mama bird sits with the babies.

  Ⓑ Papa and Mama bird look for food and sit with the babies.

  Ⓒ Papa bird looks for food, and Mama bird sits with the babies.

10. Look at the web about frogs. Which detail goes in the web?

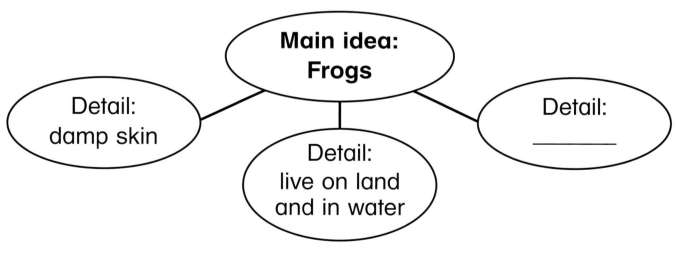

  Ⓐ a sunny day

  Ⓑ toads

  Ⓒ strong back legs

11. Read the lines from "Animal Parts."

> Birds have wings to help them fly.
> Koalas use their arms and legs to climb.
> Fish have fins to help them swim.

Why do fish need fins?

Ⓐ   They live in water.

Ⓑ   They live on land.

Ⓒ   They live in houses.

12. Which picture name begins with the same sound as the picture in the box?

Ⓐ

Ⓑ

Ⓒ

13. Read the sentence from "Amazing Animals."

> The arms of an octopus have strong muscles for catching prey.

What question should you ask after you read the sentence?

(A)   How many muscles does a whale have?

(B)   Are my muscles strong?

(C)   What does an octopus use its arms for?

14. Which are <u>different</u>?

      (A)   (B)   (C)

15. You come to a word you do not know. What should you do?

(A)   Sound out the word.

(B)   Stop reading.

(C)   Circle the capital letters.

Student _____ Date _____

THEME 16

Student Theme Progress Test Record

Skills Tested	Item Numbers (cross out numbers for items answered incorrectly)	Student Score	Criterion Score	If the student scored less than the Criterion Score, use these Reteaching Tools:
Comprehension Use Fix-Up Strategies: Decoding Word Parts	1 6 15	_____ of 3	2 / 3	**Use Fix-Up Strategies: Decoding Word Parts:** Comprehension Bridge 16
Monitor Understanding: Reread Text	11 13	_____ of 2	1 / 2	**Monitor Understanding: Reread Text:** Comprehension Bridge 15
Vocabulary	2 14	_____ of 2	2 / 2	**Vocabulary:** During independent reading time, review student's Vocabulary Journal and discuss how to improve the journal entries
Phonics Final Blends *nd, nt, st*	5 8	_____ of 2	1 / 2	**Final Blends *nd, nt, st*:** Whole Class Charts p. 139 Teacher's Guide p. 502
ch, wh Digraphs	3 12	_____ of 2	1 / 2	***ch, wh* Digraphs:** Whole Class Charts p. 144 Teacher's Guide p. 518
Writing: Process Writing Process: Editing	7	_____ of 1	1 / 1	**Process: Editing:** Writing Chart 46 Writing Bridge 31
Organizational Pattern: Main Idea and Details	10	_____ of 1	1 / 1	**Organizational Pattern: Main Idea and Details:** Writing Chart 47, 48 Writing Bridge 32
Writing: Grammar Join Simple Sentences with *and*	9	_____ of 1	1 / 1	**Join Simple Sentences with *and*:** Writing Resource Guide p. 31 Writer's Handbook p. 6
Review Simple and Compound Sentences	4	_____ of 1	1 / 1	**Simple and Compound Sentences:** Writing Resource Guide p. 32 Writer's Handbook p. 6
		_____ / 15	11 / 15	

Answer Key

1. A   2. C   3. A   4. C   5. B   6. B   7. A   8. B   9. C   10. C

11. A   12. B   13. C   14. B   15. A

Name _____   Date _____

Fill in the circle next to your answer.

1. Which picture name has the same ending sounds as **sell**?

Ⓐ   Ⓑ   Ⓒ

2. Which two smaller words are used to make the
picture word?

cup + sweet   ice + cake   cup + cake

Ⓐ   Ⓑ   Ⓒ

3. What word has the same ending sounds as the
picture word?

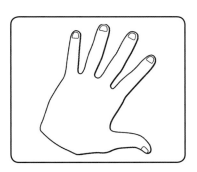

bend   cent   bump

Ⓐ   Ⓑ   Ⓒ

4. How would you end a letter to a friend?

Ⓐ Dear Friend,

Ⓑ Yours truly,

Ⓒ Hello!

5. What word shows when something happens in a story?

blue
Ⓐ

next
Ⓑ

and
Ⓒ

6. What word has the same beginning sound as the picture word?

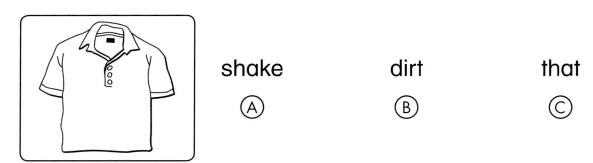

shake
Ⓐ

dirt
Ⓑ

that
Ⓒ

7. Which picture name rhymes with **tar**?

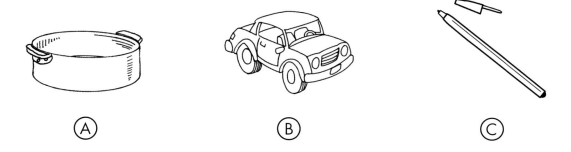

Ⓐ   Ⓑ   Ⓒ

8. What does the word <u>wandered</u> mean?

The bear woke up. She <u>wandered</u> out of the cave.

Ⓐ   dug deep

Ⓑ   walked around

Ⓒ   ate berries

9. Read the sentences.

> Joseph eats his lunch. Oh, no! He gets ketchup on his shirt.

What can you write to fix Joseph's problem?

Ⓐ   He washes his shirt. It's clean now!

Ⓑ   He doesn't eat the rest of his lunch.

Ⓒ   He is sad. He can't find a napkin.

Read the story. Fill in the circle next to your answer.

Say Hello to Socks

I told my mom and dad that I wanted a snake.

"No," said my mom. "No more about snakes."

I waited a day. I told them I wanted an ant farm.

"No," said my dad. "What if the ants got out?"

I waited some more. Then I told them that I wanted a frog.

"Oh, Henry!" my mom said. "What kind of pets are snakes and ants and frogs? Do you want a different kind of pet? Do you want one that you can pet and hold?"

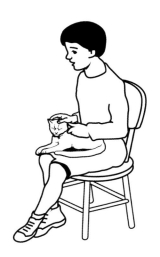

I told my mom that I did want that kind of pet. That is how I got the pet I really wanted. Say hello to Socks!

10. What kind of pet did Henry really want?

      (A)   ants

      (B)   frog

      (C)   cat

11. What is an important detail in this story?

      (A)   Henry wants a pet that he can pet and hold.

      (B)   Ants can get out of an ant farm.

      (C)   A pet can be named "Socks."

12. Read the sentences. Choose the sentence that comes last in the story.

      (A)   Henry names the cat Socks.

      (B)   Mom asks Henry if he would like a pet to hold.

      (C)   Henry gets a pet cat.

Read the poem. Fill in the circle next to your answer.

The Moon

What I love about the night

Is that the moon lights up the sky.

It just seems to hang there

While the stars stand by.

Sometimes the moon is a big ball.

Other times, it's just a little slice.

But I almost always find it,

And to me it looks so nice!

13. Which word rhymes with **night**?

  nice   net   sight

  Ⓐ   Ⓑ   Ⓒ

14. Where is the moon seen?

    Ⓐ   on a plate

    Ⓑ   in the sky

    Ⓒ   under water

15. Read the lines from "The Moon."

> What I love about the night
> Is that the moon lights up the sky.
> It just seems to hang there
> While the stars stand by.

Which two words rhyme?

    Ⓐ   sky, there

    Ⓑ   sky, by

    Ⓒ   stand, by

16. Which picture tells you about the poem?

    Ⓐ   Ⓑ   Ⓒ

Read the story. Fill in the circle next to your answer.

Number Game

Do you like to play games? Do you need to practice adding numbers? Make a number game! This game is easy and fun.

What to Do

1. Find an old calendar, scissors, and 6 clothespins.

2. Cut numbers 1 to 12 from a calendar. Mix them up.

3. Pick two numbers. Clip them together with a clothespin. Do this until you have used all the clothespins.

4. Play the game.

How to Play the Game (2 players)

1. Player 1 picks a clothespin. He or she adds the numbers. Then Player 1 writes down the numbers and his or her answer.

2. Player 2 does the same thing.

3. Play until there are no clothespins left.

4. Ask a teacher or parent to check the adding of both players.

17. Where do the numbers in the game come from?

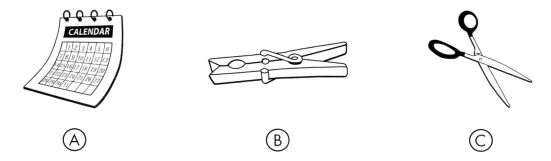

Ⓐ   Ⓑ   Ⓒ

18. Who probably wins at the end of the game?

Ⓐ   The player who doesn't add numbers.

Ⓑ   The player who clips the numbers together.

Ⓒ   The player who adds the most numbers correctly.

19. You do not know how to say the word <u>clothespin</u>. How would you break it apart?

     cl othe spin   clothes pin   clot hes pin

         Ⓐ   Ⓑ   Ⓒ

20. Which word goes on the line?

     If the adding is not correct, the player made a _____.

        mistake   contact   cloud

       Ⓐ   Ⓑ   Ⓒ

Read the story. Fill in the circle next to your answer.

Breakfast on the Farm

Farmer Dodd went out to feed the animals. "Would you like some oatmeal?" he asked Horse.

"No, thanks," said Horse. "I would like just oats. Chomp! Chomp!" He ate until he was full.

"Would you like some potatoes?" Farmer Dodd asked Pig.

"No, thanks," said Pig. "I would like just the peels. Oink! Oink!" She ate until she was full.

"Would you like some bread?" Farmer Dodd asked Chicken.

"No, thanks," said Chicken. "I would like just grain. Cluck. Cluck." She ate until she was full.

Farmer Dodd had oatmeal, potatoes, and bread. What should he do? He sat and ate oatmeal, potatoes, and bread.

"It is time for breakfast!" called his wife.

"No, thanks," said Farmer Dodd. "I am full!"

21. Which word sounds like what it means?

chomp
Ⓐ

bread
Ⓑ

time
Ⓒ

22. What makes this story make-believe?

Ⓐ   Farm animals talk.

Ⓑ   A farmer feeds a pig.

Ⓒ   A horse eats oats.

23. Read the lines from "Breakfast on the Farm."

"No, thanks," said Pig. "I would like just the peels. Oink! Oink!" She ate until she was full.

What should you do if you do not understand this?

Ⓐ   Find words that rhyme.

Ⓑ   Ask yourself questions.

Ⓒ   Spell each word.

Read the story. Fill in the circle next to your answer.

Rosa's Lunchbox

"What is in your lunch?" Chuck asked. "Let's trade!"

Rosa opened her lunchbox. She smiled. "I have some rice from last night. I did not know there was any left. My grandpa ate a lot of rice. He said it was the best." She laughed. "I do not want to trade my rice."

Chuck asked, "Will you trade for my apple?"

Rosa smiled. "My sister helped me pick out the bananas at the store," she said. "It was funny. She said we were monkeys. I do not want to trade my banana."

Chuck asked, "Do you have any food you will trade?"

Rosa said, "It seems like I have my family with me in my lunchbox. I do not want to trade. But I will share."

"You do have a lot of stories about your family in there!" Chuck said.

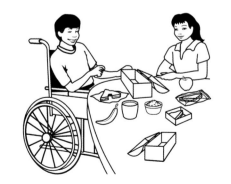

The children ate their own lunches.

24. How is Chuck's lunch different from Rosa's?

    Ⓐ   Chuck has an apple. Rosa has a banana.

    Ⓑ   Chuck has rice. Rosa has rice.

    Ⓒ   Chuck has a banana. Rosa has a family.

25. Where does this story take place?

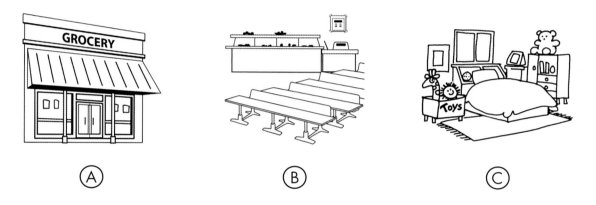

          Ⓐ   Ⓑ   Ⓒ

26. What did Rosa have for dinner last night?

    Ⓐ   rice

    Ⓑ   an apple

    Ⓒ   a lunchbox

Read the story. Fill in the circle next to your answer.

A Tasty Treat

Many people go to New Jersey each summer. They swim. They ride in boats. They play in the waves. They play in the sand. And many people eat a tasty treat called taffy! Taffy is a kind of candy.

It is sometimes called saltwater taffy. How did it get that name? No one knows for sure. But here is what some people think.

Long ago, a man was selling tasty taffy. Each bit of taffy had paper around it. The man had a stand near the <u>ocean</u>. Wind came up. Big waves splashed on the beach. Salt water landed on the taffy. The man called it saltwater taffy. The taffy is not made from salt water. At one time, it just had salt water on the paper!

27. Which of these is an <u>ocean</u>?

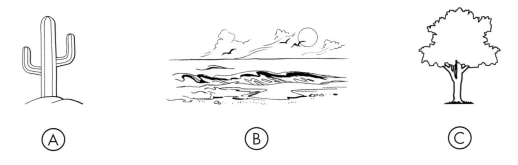

Ⓐ   Ⓑ   Ⓒ

28. Read the sentence from "A Tasty Treat."

> Long ago, a man was selling tasty taffy.

Which words have the same beginning sound?

long ago
Ⓐ

was selling
Ⓑ

tasty taffy
Ⓒ

29. What is the story mainly about?

Ⓐ what saltwater taffy looks like

Ⓑ what saltwater taffy tastes like

Ⓒ how saltwater taffy got its name

30. Which sentence is most important to the story?

Ⓐ Taffy is a kind of candy.

Ⓑ No one knows for sure.

Ⓒ Many people go to New Jersey each summer.

Student _____   Date _____

End-of-Year Review Test Record

Comprehension

Cross out numbers for items answered incorrectly.

Make Connections	17	Determine Importance: Main Idea	29
Determine Importance	30	Synthesize: Retell	11
Infer	26	Infer: Conclusions	18
Monitor Understanding	23	Monitor Understanding: Reread Text	10
Make Connections: Compare and Contrast Information	24	Use Fix-Up Strategies: Decoding Word Parts	19
Ask Questions: Meaning	14		
Create Images	16		

If student has difficulty with Comprehension, use the Comprehension Bridges.

Total Comprehension Score _____ / 12

Target Skill

Distinguish Fantasy from Reality	22	Identify Story Structure	12
Recognize Rhythm and Rhyme	15	Identify Setting	25
Recognize Alliteration	28	Recognize Onomatopoeia	21

If student has difficulty with Target Skills, use the Teacher's Guide lessons.

Total Target Skill Score _____ / 6

Vocabulary

8   20   27

If student has difficulty with Vocabulary, review student's Vocabulary Journal.

Total Vocabulary Score _____ / 3

Phonics

th, *sh* Digraphs	6	Compound Words	2
ill, *ell* Word Families	1	*r*-Controlled Vowels	7
ie, *ight* Word Families	13	Final Blends *nd*, *nt*, *st*	3

If student has difficulty with Phonics, use the Whole Class Charts and Teacher's Guide lessons.

Total Phonics Score _____ / 6

Writing: Process Writing

Form: Letter	4	Organizational Pattern: Problem and Solution	9
Organizational Pattern: Sequence	5		

If student has difficulty with Writing, use the Writing Bridges.

Total Writing: Process Writing Score _____ / 3

Total Score _____ / 30

Answer Key

1. C	4. B	7. B	10. C	13. C	16. C	19. B	22. A	25. B	28. C
2. C	5. B	8. B	11. A	14. B	17. A	20. A	23. B	26. A	29. C
3. A	6. A	9. A	12. A	15. B	18. C	21. A	24. A	27. B	30. A

High-Frequency Word Assessments

Use the High-Frequency Word Assessments to assess a child's ability to recognize and read high-frequency words for each theme.

Administer the assessment one-on-one at the end of each theme. Photocopy the page. Point to one word at a time and have the child say the word aloud. If the child stalls on a word, silently count to five and then say the word. Move on to the next word.

Use the High-Frequency Word Assessment Tracking Form on page 177 to record student progress and make notes about student responses. Record words that students didn't recognize and return to them during a future assessment.

was	from	have	but	what
one	will	some	into	out

put	today	so	went	make
teacher	has	no	grow	now

day	did	little	very	park
then	good	house	I'm	it's

land	of	oh	them	want
that	need	came	two	children

milk	by	or	there	more
made	an	other	way	every

THEME 6

first	who	live	after	ask
book	thing	can't	don't	boy

THEME 7

cat	eat	just	bus	people
yes	saw	man	think	didn't

THEME 8

right	old	same	door	tell
find	new	work	well	read

still   got   us   next   something

that's   stop   feet   took   thought

miss   talk   fish   sit   morning

pet   ran   shout   take   were

please   room   Mrs.   Mr.   sleep

thank   woman   their   does   anything

THEME 12

sun	about	across	blue	again
air	always	black	past	along

THEME 13

they	also	cold	easy	care
ate	began	long	end	around

THEME 14

between	city	begin	cut	behind
know	another	boat	each	couldn't

close   bad   add   call   catch

as   best   animal   enough   everything

before   brother   done   any   beautiful

clean   bring   fall   better   everyone

High-Frequency Word Assessment Tracking Form

Student _____

For each theme's high-frequency word assessment, record the words students did not recognize. You may want to return to missed words during the next theme's one-on-one assessment. Record notes about student responses.

Theme	Date	High-Frequency Words Missed	Notes About Student Responses	Score
1				___/10
2				___/10
3				___/10
4				___/10
5				___/10
6				___/10
7				___/10
8				___/10
9				___/10
10				___/10
11				___/10
12				___/10
13				___/10
14				___/10
15				___/10
16				___/10

Ongoing Test Practice Answer Key

Theme 1
S. B
1. A
2. B
3. C
4. A

Theme 2
S. B
1. A
2. B
3. A
4. C

Theme 3
S. A
1. C
2. B
3. A
4. C

Theme 4
S. B
1. C
2. B
3. A
4. A

Theme 5
S. B
1. B
2. C
3. A
4. A

Theme 6
S. C
1. A
2. A
3. B
4. C

Theme 7
S. B
1. C
2. A
3. B
4. C

Theme 8
S. C
1. A
2. B
3. B
4. C

Theme 9
S. A
1. C
2. C
3. B
4. A

Theme 10
S. B
1. C
2. C
3. A
4. B

Theme 11
S. B
1. A
2. B
3. C
4. A

Theme 12
S. B
1. A
2. B
3. A
4. C

Theme 13
S. B
1. B
2. C
3. A
4. C

Theme 14
S. A
1. B
2. C
3. C
4. A

Theme 15
S. B
1. A
2. C
3. A
4. C

Theme 16
S. A
1. B
2. B
3. A
4. C

Phonemic Awareness Intervention

Assess these four key Phonemic Awareness skills for grade 1. Provide daily instruction until students have mastered each skill.

Phoneme Segmentation

Assessment

Say: *I am going to say a word. After I say the word, I want you to say each sound of the word that you hear. If I say* <u>lot</u>, *you would say /l/ /o/ /t/. Be sure to say each of the three sounds separately.*

Say: *Now I want you to try one. I want you to say each sound of the word that you hear:* <u>hop</u>. (/h/ /o/ /p/)

If the child answers correctly, continue by administering the five items below. Ask the child to say each sound of the word.

If the child has difficulty identifying each sound, repeat the word *hop* and then say the three sounds. Tell the child that the sounds in the word *hop* are /h/ /o/ /p/.

Words Read by the Teacher

1. yes (/y/ /e/ /s/)
2. dig (/d/ /i/ /g/)
3. sip (/s/ /i/ /p/)
4. ten (/t/ /e/ /n/)
5. hum (/h/ /u/ /m/)

If the child has difficulty with phoneme segmentation, use the instruction below.

Instruction

Show children how to segment sounds in words. *Listen as I say each sound in the word* pat: *I will hold up a finger for each sound I say: /p/ /a/ /t/. There are three sounds in this word. What is the word?* (pat)

Now you do it with me. Follow the routine for the word *man*. Then have children work in pairs to segment and say the number of sounds in these words: *tan, cat, mat, can,* challenge: *stop.* Continue daily instruction with other 3-phoneme and 4-phoneme words until the skill is mastered.

Phoneme Blending

Assessment

Say: *I will say the sounds of a word. Put the sounds together and tell me what the word is. For example, if I say /d/ /o/ /g/, what would you say?* (dog)

If the child answers correctly, continue by administering the five items below. Ask the child to put the word sounds together to say the word.

If the child has difficulty putting the sounds together, say the three sounds again and then blend them together to make the word *dog*.

Phonemes Read by the Teacher
1. /m/ /o/ /p/ (mop)
2. /k/ /u/ /t/ (cut)
3. /b/ /a/ /t/ (bat)
4. /f/ /e/ /d/ (fed)
5. /r/ /i/ /b/ (rib)

If the child has difficulty with phoneme blending, use the instruction below.

Instruction

Tell children that you are going to say some sounds and then blend the sounds to form a word. Model phoneme blending for children. *Listen as I say each sound: /s/ /a/ /t/. Let's blend the sounds together: /s/-/a /-/t/. What is the word?* (sat)

Repeat with *cap*. Have pairs blend the sounds for these words: *fan, map, mat, lap*. Continue daily instruction with other 3-phoneme and 4-phoneme words until the skill is mastered.

Phoneme Addition and Deletion

Assessment (Addition)

Say: *I am going to say a word. Then I am going to say a sound. I want you to add the sound to the beginning of the word to make a new word. For example, if I say the word <u>ad</u> and the sound /m/, you would say <u>mad</u>. Now you try to do the same thing. If I say the word <u>all</u>, what would the word be if you add the /t/ sound to the beginning?* (tall)

If the child answers correctly, administer the five items below. Ask the child to add the sound to the word. If the child has difficulty adding the sound to the beginning of the word, explain that adding the sound /t/ to the word *all* makes the new word *tall*.

Words and Sounds Read by the Teacher

1. oat /c/ (coat) **2.** all /b/ (ball) **3.** age /p/ (page) **4.** oil /s/ (soil) **5.** at /p/ (pat)

If the child has difficulty with phoneme addition, use the instruction below.

Assessment (Deletion)

Say: *I am going to say a word. Then I am going to say a part of that word. I want you to say the word back to me without that part. For example, if I say the word <u>boil</u> and then ask you to say the word without the /b/ sound, you would say <u>oil</u>. Now you try it. If I say the word <u>rice</u>, what would the word be without the /r/ sound?* (ice)

If the child answers correctly, continue by administering the five items below. If the child has difficulty deleting the sound from the word, explain that without the /r/ sound in the word *rice*, the word would be *ice*. Say the sound and the word.

Words and Sounds Read by the Teacher

1. band /b/ (and) **2.** sold /s/ (old) **3.** mat /m/ (at) **4.** link /l/ (ink) **5.** heat /h/ (eat)

If the child has difficulty with phoneme deletion, use the instruction below.

Instruction

Listen as I say this word: ape. *Now let's add /k/ to the beginning of* ape. *The word is* cape. *Say each sound with me: /k/, ape. The word is cape. What is the word?* (cape) Then have children add /m/ to *ade* to make *made*.

Now I will say a word as you listen to the beginning and ending sounds. Then we'll leave off the beginning sound. The word is cage. *The beginning sound is /k/. What is the beginning sound?* (k) *Now I'll leave off the /k/ sound. The new word is* age. *Repeat the routine, having children delete the beginning sounds of the following words:* gate, tape, wage. *Continue daily instruction with other phonemes that can be added to and deleted from words until the skill is mastered.*

Phoneme Substitution

Assessment

Say: *I am going to say a word, and then I am going to say one sound that is a part of the word. Then I will tell you to change the sound to a new sound. I want you to say the word back to me, changing the first sound to the second sound. For example, if I say the word* can, *and then I say change the /c/ sound to the /m/ sound, you would say* man. *Now you try the same thing. The word is* toy. *What would the word be if you changed the /t/ sound to the /b/ sound?* (boy)

If the child answers correctly, administer the five items below. Ask the child to tell you what the word would be if you changed the first sound to the second sound.

If the child has difficulty substituting one sound for another, explain that if the /t/ sound in the word *toy* was changed to the /b/ sound, the word would be *boy*.

Words and Sounds Read by the Teacher
1. gap /g/ /k/ (cap)
2. seed /s/ /w/ (weed)
3. walk /w/ /t/ (talk)
4. jam /j/ /h/ (ham)
5. book /b/ /l/ (look)

If the child has difficulty substituting phonemes, use the instruction below.

Instruction

Model phoneme substitution with children: *Listen as I say this word*: cap. Cap *begins with the /k/ sound. Let's say the sound together: /k/. Now let's change the /k/ sound to a new sound: /l/. Say it with me, /l/. The new word is* lap. *What is the new word?* (lap). *Now, instead of /l/, say /m/. What's the new word?* (map) Guide children to substitute the beginning sounds of these words: *cot, hot, got; bed, fed, led.*

Listen as I say this word: clock. *Listen for the vowel sound in* clock: /o/. *Repeat the /o/ sound and stretch it out:* o-o-o-o. *Now let's change the /o/ sound to a new sound: /i/. Say it with me, /i/. The new word is* click. *What is the new word?* (click). *Now, instead of /i/, say /u/. What's the new word?* (cluck) Guide children to substitute the medial vowel sounds of these words: *black, block; slid, sled; clap, clip.*

Continue daily instruction with other words that have phonemes that can be substituted until the skill is mastered.